The Untidy Season

The Untidy Season

An Anthology of Nebraska Women Poets

Heidi Hermanson, Liz Kay, Jen Lambert,
and Sarah McKinstry-Brown, Editors

The Backwaters Press

Copyright © 2013 by The Backwaters Press
Cover design by Bristol Creative, www.bristolcreative.com
Interior design by Susan Ramundo, susan@srdesktopservices.com
Cover artwork, "Liquor, Worms, Movies," by Heidi Hermanson, © 2013,
    used by permission of the artist.

The Backwaters Press
3502 N 52nd Street
Omaha, Nebraska 68104-3506

Greg Kosmicki and Rich Wyatt, Editors
www.thebackwaterspress.org
thebackwaterspress@gmail.com

First Printing, September 2013

Printed in the United States of America

ISBN: 978-1-935218-32-6

Contents

Preface

What you're holding in your hands at this moment, though bound and decidedly tidy, is the culmination of many heated and maddening discussions.

One night, during a particularly long and difficult editors meeting, I remember looking across the dining room table at my fellow editor's 7-year-old daughter. This little girl sat quietly drawing while her mother and the rest of us read and argued our way through a pile of poems. Knowing that this young girl was witness to a group of women arguing and debating over something as small as a poem was a comfort to me, and it ought to be to you, too. Here was proof that, as our fellow poet Ted Kooser has said, in poetry, as in life, "The large is present in the small." This small act of us putting together an anthology has much larger implications. The creation of this anthology gave a 7-year-old girl (one who has turned out to be a blossoming poet) the experience of witnessing strong, creative women have it out over art, specifically the words of other strong, creative women.

The arguments we had around that dining room table (and beyond) are proof that the voices in this anthology cannot be pinned down, proof that when you open this book you'll discover a landscape that houses a multitude of voices and visions, many of them conflicting and contradictory.

Turn the page and you'll find Nebraska women poets whose experiences are not as tidy as the rows of corn and rolling plains that define much of our landscape. Turn the page and you'll find poems that are bent on breaking and mending your heart in the same breath.

My Great-Great Uncle is Conscripted into the War

Lucy Adkins

When the soldiers came,
the boys were out in the field,
Hans leading the mule,
Herbert behind the plow.
Sixty years later my cousin told the story,
and I imagine it was May,
swallows wheeling in the lowland sky,
apple blossoms drifting to the dark
curl of earth.
And it was a day to be alive:
the earth opening up,
rich smell of mule and hard work.
So when they said they must fight
for the Fatherland,
Hans said *No way in hell.*
Then the creak of leathers
as the mule shifted;
explosion of birds
when the gun came out.
Herbert went with them—
left the plow in the field,
left behind his brother, dead.
His children remembered
and passed down the story;
and when they could,
they got on a boat
and came to America.

The Untidy Season

Turkey Buzzards

Lucy Adkins

Five or six blocks from our house
a family of turkey buzzards
has settled in,
found a craggy tree in someone's backyard
and declared it home.
They've been encouraged to go,
their habit of regurgitating food disgusting,
the way they have of hunkering on a tree limb
and looking down on you.

But they remain.
We've seen them a lot
these past few days
soaring in lazy circles
over 40th and Sheridan,
intersecting in arcs,
then gliding over
our house.

They are only birds.
They are only seeking out the thermals,
rising and falling on the currents
as they are wont to do.
Influenza has been bad this year,
and in general, times are hard.
My husband says he wishes they'd fly
a little farther to the south.

It's all a joke, really,
these birds of cartoons and old westerns,
and in reality, their flight is beautiful
as death might seem
when you're not there close,
as death might be,
hovering and circling
and always out there.

How to Write a Poem
(from conversations with my dad)

Sana Amoura-Patterson

If you want to write a poem about my experience
you will have to describe how a son was born
into a loving atmosphere between the village of al-Tira
and the city of Haifa. You would have to include
his good relations with olive farmers and businessmen.
Remind your audience that he was brought up
secure and with a lot of ambition
and tell how he was given an education
so he could become somebody and have all
the means to accomplish his family's dreams.

Then tell them that his education was disrupted
by immigrations to Jordan and then America
where he washed his dinner dishes in the bathtub
and his young wife learned to cook without an oven
or spices. You should include that they were happy
and hopeful. They named their first child *Aida*
which means *to return*. Shoveling sand and starting
school again was another beginning. Then tell
about the four children later when he lost his wife
and then gained a new wife and more children
and you know all of that stuff in-between and after.

You put in the dots of course. You write it into proper
English or poetry. I'm dumb.
Poetry is something I like, but I never got the knack.
I use it a lot when I speak, but I was never able to put it together.
I was serious. I was the eldest son of an eldest son.
I recited great Arab poets, but I was dry myself.
In fact, I was never attracted to art or music.

But what about the Arabic tapes in the car?
The minor melancholy sounds we were forbidden to touch?
The songs you sang to when you'd drive us to school?

Oh those? Noise. I just wanted the company.

Bessma and Country Music

Sana Amoura-Patterson

When Lyle Lovett sings
I think of my cousin's feet
thick from walking on concrete
carrying four kids and a husband
who walked out across the bridge
from Jordan to Palestine
looking for work eight years ago.
I haven't seen him for two visits
and I stopped asking when he'll return
and my sister Jean and I gave up
trying to understand how
my cousins buy food.

Instead, we take our turns
smoking from the water pipe
on top of my aunt's roof
while our shirts begin to wiggle
and flap as the warm afternoon
breeze picks up.
We sit on chairs held together
with wires that used to hang
in closets and a couch that used
to be inside. Now bricks
help hold up the unsteady legs
and springs poke through the place
where my uncle used to sit.

My cousins move in heavy clothes
between their apartments
and their mother's house.
All the men are gone, so we serve
ourselves tea with leaves, thick
coffee, nuts and sticky sweets.
We talk but cannot understand
our language. We nod

and smile and try to act out
our meanings, but Bessma and Emil
cannot comprehend why Jean and I buy
books and worry about work. They ask
about Texas—a place we've never been.
They don't understand why we would
overlook a state so big and free
as broad as Bessma's feet.

Every morning is like this:
the sun lifts off the sand to dry
our clothes on the line. We roll
grape leaves and stuff cabbages
cut tomatoes and pray. And when
it's dusk the children crowd
on to the roof and fly
kites of sticks and strings that tangle
in TV antennas until little Mahmoud
sets them free again to hang
suspended over the sand
and ruins, homes and women
on top of roofs.

Over kites and bubbling water
the heat and the light retreat
to the Mavericks and Lovett,
Bessma and Emil,
my sister and me
dancing between
the wildly flapping
clothes on the line.

Looking Away

Sana Amoura-Patterson

It happens sometimes:
You look down, and when you look
back up, the drive-in theater,
where you spent prom drinking beer
with your friends in your '73 Montego
is now an Albertson's where your
student is the checker eyeing
over the items you will later stuff
under your bathroom sink.
Or a new Baptist church, with elaborate
stained-glass windows, springs out
of a cornfield on Sorenson Parkway
on your way to a meeting.
Or your daughter, who suddenly
learned to talk, scolds you
for driving too fast when you're
late to school, and your hair is still
wet and you realize you're wearing one blue
shoe and one black and you don't
have time to stop back home.

So, Dad, I wonder—if I resist looking away
and keep my eyes fixed on the brown spots
on your hand, can I keep you to the end
unchanged?

I Didn't Know

Sana Amoura-Patterson

I didn't know I loved
the smoke from your pipe
your bent form washing dishes
watching you wait
for water to boil

your worn blue and green bathrobe
the stains on your teeth
the brown spots on your hands
your disgust whenever I cried

I didn't know I loved
the stack of small plastic containers
you kept by your chair
to hold miniature chocolate bars, tobacco,
and dried apricots

The stories you told again and again
about donkeys and onions
thinly veiled lessons
we called lectures.

I didn't know I loved
the old man hats you wore
that still smell like you
the straw hat you'd
tip up on your forehead
whenever we went boating

I didn't know I loved
trips to Sam's Club
pushing the cart
or the stockpile of paper
products in your garage

The Untidy Season

I didn't know I loved
the straight lines
you used to cross off tasks
the wet Ziploc bags you recycled
the turkeys you'd buy on sale
to crowd your freezer
waiting for you to feel generous

I didn't know I loved
the sweet tobacco that stained your fingers
the suits you donned like costumes
whenever you went to the bank
burns on the carpet
circling your chair

The jagged breathing
I wanted to end
the harsh commands
and bells you rang to call us

I didn't know I loved
your round forehead
until I kissed you
        the heat already receding
as the nurses awkwardly crowded
your doorway
waiting to take you away

Castell' Alfero

Mary Avidano

Remembering a story
told to my mother-in-law
by her mother-in-law

I.

The ancestors of my children
(on their father's father's side)
came from a Piemontese village
named for its castle of iron.
Castell' Alfero—I should want
to see in every light those
tile roofs at the foot of the tall
stern tower, there in Piemonte,
at the feet of snowy mountains.

II.

Rosina, imprisoned at nineteen
in the iron castle of an arranged
marriage, must have looked out
and past the moonlit vineyards.
She lost four babies in Italy, it
was later said among the others,
the eight who lived. The father,
Angelo Domenico Avidano, who
was no angel, it is true, provided
for his family nonetheless. He
heard talk of better prospects,
booked their passage to America.

III.

In November, then, of the fifth
year into the century, Rosina
looked back for a last time to
Castell' Alfero's rooftops, and
to the babies' graves. First in
Hell's Kitchen, then, when they
had saved enough, in Queens,
the family scrabbled for work.
Years passed. One day, when
Rosina sat quietly mending,
with only her daughter-in-law
nearby, she said for no reason,
*There was a boy from the next
farm over. I would meet him
in the hedgerow between our
families' vineyards.* That was
all, and never to her daughters
did she say even so much as
this: that one love in a lifetime
lets a person see in every light.

For a Survivor

Mary Avidano

Before the Exodus from Egypt,
deep within an airless turquoise mine,
a slave took up the oppressor's tool
and with it wrote on the cavern's wall,
O God, save me. Archeologists
of modern times bring their lanterns near
to read in proto-alphabet
this prayer or cry—on walls of prison
cells, asylums, ships, the selfsame plea.
Now, my friend, you need to ask what use
I am as your companion: is it
to say you must look on the bright side—
or try at least to count your blessings?
No, I am here (and I will be here)
only to hold the light whereby you
may look and see what is written there
in your deepest heart, the primal word.

The Untidy Season

15

City Lights

Mary Avidano

> *The lamplighter was finishing his rounds.*
> —Howard Hanke

My father, rather a quiet man,
told a story only the one time,
if even then—he had so little
need, it seemed, of being understood.
Intervals of years, his silences!
Late in his life he recalled for us
that when he was sixteen, his papa
entrusted to him a wagonload
of hogs, which he was to deliver
to the train depot, a half-day's ride
from home, over a hilly dirt road.
Lightly he held the reins, light his heart,
the old horses, as ever, willing.
In town at noon he heard the station-
master say the train had been delayed,
would not arrive until that evening.
The boy could only wait. At home they'd
wait for him and worry and would place
the kerosene lamp in the window.
Thus the day had turned to dusk before
he turned about the empty wagon,
took his weary horses through the cloud
of fireflies that was the little town.
In all his years he'd never seen those
lights—he thought of this, he said, until
he and his milk-white horses came down
the last moonlit hill to home, drawn as
from a distance toward a single flame.

Babushka

Mary Avidano

> *n.* 1. A head scarf folded in a triangle and tied below the chin;
> 2. in Russia and Poland, an old woman or grandmother.

At fifteen I left my broken home
in Nebraska, entered a convent
in Chicago. This way at least I'd
always have a roof over my head,
the kindly grownups said with a sigh.
Once at the bus stop on Pulaski
a woman scolded me. Where is your
babushka? she wanted to know. So
I learned a new word that winter day.
Babushka—its syllables were as
satisfying as bread, caraway
rye the kitchen Sisters baked. "Is not
the body more than clothing?" asked our
Lord, seeing the lilies of the field.
Those first years, waiting to take the veil,
I little thought instead I'd marry,
give birth, become an old grandmother
feeding my chickens.

A Mind of Winter

Grace Bauer

I

It is difficult to love,
I think, a season felt
so deeply in the bones.

I have tried
stoic acceptance,
concentration on the beauty

to be found in gradations
of grays, browns—
all winter's colors.

I have tried a kind
of human hibernation,
but still I find myself

wishing away months
of my life, longing for
Springtime to arrive like a lover.

I want to force it
like a hothouse bulb
to blossom before its time.

II

I acknowledge
the blessings hidden in this
bleakness: the dingy

trailers rendered invisible,
the blue jay at the feeder
more brilliant for

the backdrop of gray.

III

The birds flocking
at the feeder sing

at the first real sun
we've seen in days.

The trees drip
incessantly letting go
of yesterday's hard shining.

IV

Even memory has gone
flat, gray, so used
to silence the rare sun
can't conjure up a word
or picture worth words.

Birds flit from branch
to feeder to grass, repeat
the frantic circle. The goldfish
circle the infinite confines
of their newly cleaned bowl.

Sun slashes light, shadow,
light across the cold
room someone enters looking
for reading glasses, Scotch
tape, a pencil—some ordinary
object that has momentarily
slipped their mind.

V

Ask me and I'll tell you
I hate winter. The cold, the dark,
even the gorgeous extravagance

of snow if it lingers longer than a day.
I claim kinship with the animals
who burrow in, sleep
through the season, storing up
for better days. But human
conventions call me out
into the chilly thick of things.
I go, cursing the going.

Then some morning I spot
a cardinal in the bare locust—
its red more than red
in the grayness that surrounds.
Or on the one clear night we've seen
in weeks, the stars force my eyes
heavenward to glimpse the moon.

VI

This *storm of the century*
transforms all I know,
defamiliarizes the scene
I stare out my windows at
three days running, still
disconcerted by the everyday
covered so thickly in white.

No reason for it to remind me
of death, but it does. My own.
Lately I've been imagining it
at the oddest times. Spring
a week away and we are
hunkered down, immobilized
by the unexpected, which we
should learn by now to expect.

I have to admit it *is* beautiful,
though, like much beauty, less
than convenient. Like death—

my own or anyone's, arriving
before we're quite prepared.
I am mesmerized now by the light
on the snow.
      No. That's not it.
Not exactly.

It's the birds
flying frantically around the seed
I've tossed out. It's the shadows
made by all that light.

Great Plains Prayer

Grace Bauer

Bless us, oh Lord,
and this our Jell-O. Our corn,
our steaks and kolaches.
Our heat indexes. Our wind chills.
Our sunsets and horizons.
Our endless waves of grain and grass.
Our ancestors who started out
for the coast but stopped halfway.
Our nostalgia for their calico,
their sod, their old homesteads.
Our denial of the meth labs
that have taken their place.
Bless our perseverance.
Our unerring politeness.
Our red state politics
and our white, white bread.
Bless our dubious status
as *tornado alley*, as *flyover zone*
and bless all those who fly over,
as well as those of us who, out of
choice or necessity or inertia—
forgive us, we know not why or what
we've done—but, by God, stayed.

Drowned

Katie Berger

Today brings more rain. My hands
a small room with no room
as they anchor
the feel better balloon
to the world.

The nurse said yesterday.
The clean sheets are the smooth sand
the river hasn't reached.

The news said floods come
once every 500 years. You were
once years.

The river flowed backward
in my dream
but I will not sleep.

Of Radishes and Bees

Judy Brackett

I heard them arrive, awakened in the middle
of an about-to-fall-into-the-river dream—
a great whoosh, a splash—
a boulder or yours truly, falling
pell-mell,
tumble-bumble
into the Yuba.
3 a.m. I chalked it up to three glasses of pinot grigio
and slipped back into the dream.

Next morning I saw the bees,
a science-fictiony scene, congregations
clumping, engulfing the blue hibiscus
next to the back fence. I tiptoed toward them,
tens of thousands of bee eyes upon me—
an electric, shimmery, hummery topiary.

Sinking into the grass a few feet away,
I watched and listened. Minutes passed, half an hour or so.
The bees thrummed, Smitty's dog barked, butterflies flitted
from bush to bush, skirting the swarm. Happy, I started
to whistle a tune, and the bee throng
swelled, the hum turned angry.
I could die, be stung a million times,
be carried off whole, enswarmed
in a hot, waxy, bombilating bee-loud cloud.

Holding my breath, wrapping arms around knees,
making myself small, I sighed as the bees
drew themselves in again and softened their song.
I daydreamed, remembering the childhood day
I'd spent stretched out in the dirt, sweating and watching
my radishes grow. I thought I could see
the little sprouts smidge up and up.
A few days later, I skipped out with my own round basket

to pull some up, eager for radishes dipped in salt.
Gone, just bits of green and stirred-up dirt.
Darned rabbits, my mother said.

The sun climbed, the sprinklers sprinkled, the bees
hung there, hummed there. I thought of calling someone
to come watch with me, thought of putting up a sign—
No bees allowed. No rabbits either.
Finally, I went into the house for tea
and strawberries, toast and honey,
I read, baked muffins, wrote a letter, napped.

Back outside, late afternoon, the bees
were gone. Hibiscus tissue-petals covered the grass,
a perfect quilt, an invitation.
The summer air was still humming.

A Softer Lens

Debora Bray

Bundled in a headscarf and wooly coat,
her bangs are free and blowing.
The snowy ground behind
her rises to the tracks
that split the picture in two—
craggy branches out of focus
in the distance.

An eight-year-old girl is the focus
of the black-and-white photograph.
She is my mother,
yet unlike my mother.
Contrasting
like a negative of the impenetrable
woman I remember.

Strange how lives develop
from such sparse beginnings.
Depot for a home,
trains reel,
clackety-clack across the front yard.

Migration

Becky Breed

The glint through the curtain
falls like a white ribbon across his cheek,
the rest recessed in shadow.
His neck a turkey wattle,
excess skin once robust, full—
reduced,
the color of parchment.

Every day, something changes.
Hands that once held pliers, a saw,
now instead grip empty sheets.
I keep touching him
on his chest, his leg, foot,
in front of me he is disappearing.
Bleached covers flattened,
the shape of a man slowly erodes.
Storms he has suffered
finally sweeping him away.

They tied him to the bed, the
morphine dreams left him flying
chasing blackbirds in the night.
Now he is one of them,
his face gaunt, pointed, a beak,
his ruffled bed, a nest of twigs.

Surface Tack

Kate Brooke

Chefs are known to keep
secrets, and how better
than to let the label slide
slowly from the glass, to know
Coriander from Cumin by a sticky
feel to the jar, the Fenugreek
lid dusty from occasional use. Striped
Fennel gives itself away, and anyone
can tell Cardamom but the letters
beg stenciling onto the can.
What can I say? He is the best
cook I know. Last night over
a casual risotto I thought
I spotted a trace of Turmeric
on his wrist.

Pregunta

Jill Burkey

Winter whittles things down to hard bark
against harsh air in the bright blue morning.
It is six degrees, but trees are making plans for summer—
branches of elms grow bumpy with buds.
Pregunta means *question,* as if questions breed
possibility, or pregnancy is a question only birth can answer.

I don't know what this winter wants to be about.
The rosemary and peas peek green
through snow, sapling twigs stand naked
behind rotted tomato plants—
overgrown like a well-endowed
matriarch taking up her throne.

The children sleep like trees, dishes
rest in the sink, newspapers pile up
by the fireplace, clothes fill every
basket and wait, like falling snow
filling spaces between trees.

In March, I might miss buds emerging
from themselves, but in April I will look out
this window at puffy, papery elm seeds.
All summer long we will uproot
resolute seedlings beneath their mothers' eyes,
their question answered.

When our children finally bend us
to their will and we empty our lives
into theirs, they will slip away into their own,
and then what question can I ask
in this perfect, but empty, house?

Why Men Love Hardware Stores

Jill Burkey

Disoriented from wives and work,
    men are lured to the magic of Ace,
which, John Madden proclaims, is the place.

Here, among gleaming aisles of logic
    and rows of science-laden shelves,
every problem has an answer.

In this sanctuary of rules and results
    there's nothing that can't be fixed,
made new again. Nail after knob, drill

after dovetail, these things hinge a home together.
    Strength is magnified in the sexual leverage
of tools, coupling male and female ends.

If it's a good store, they'll even know him
    by name, like a lover amongst tungsten
and veneer. When he sees the sheave

of blank keys, he will remember grooves
can be duplicated. Re-entry is possible.

Blue Wheelbarrow, Green Note

Kathleen Cain

I would like to have
a blue wheelbarrow
upended in the garden
right where I left it;
and a garden big enough
to leave things
as they are
for a few days,
even a week
at a time; a place
where I could tend
a couple of rows
of Big Boy
and Early Girl tomatoes
that would eventually fit
in the palm of my hand;
so full of the taste
of salt and lemon
that all they'd need
might be a little pepper,
though maybe not. Friends
would come over
one or two at a time
to sit here with me
in the dirt, squat down
on their haunches
next to the bushes
in the sunshine and inhale
the green note
that keeps rising
and eat those tomatoes
right off the vine until
juice and seeds
dribbled down our hands
and chins, maybe
even made us laugh

to do such a childish thing.
And before the first frost
arrived I would play
tug-of-war
with those vines
and their still-verdant
weights
then hang them
dirt and all
upside down
in the basement
till those that were going to ripen
did, maybe on through
to December
if I was lucky;
and then I would
go get that blue
wheelbarrow and work
awhile and come back
and turn it over
because I was not quite
finished with whatever
it was I was doing

The Age Olfactory
(for Arlene)

Jill Carpenter

The vinegar smell of urine
in your lap
in the nursing home makes me want to leave
get the stench out of my clothes, nostrils, hair
like the smoke and grease of pancake houses
clings to cooks and customers

Still I stay
feeding you spoonfuls of blender beans
asking you if you remember putting up strawberry jam
like the strawberry sauce on your ice cream
I sneak you some coffee and wipe your chin
adjust your bib
"Remember how you used to garden
wearing gloves, a tattered straw hat, rolled up jeans?"
This farm woman, an American icon
"Remember how you fought the weeds?"
I do. The nurses do.
They saw you on your hands and knees
weeding the hallway

Your arms are cold
I push your wheelchair past the exit doors
into 90-degree sunshine
pushing past pink roses and their dusky fragrance
past tomato plants heavy with small green fruits
I tickle your nose with a tomato leaf
and strain to understand your mumbling

I remember the taste of your sliced ripe tomatoes
garden-fresh corn on the cob saturated with butter
the smell of crispy golden fried chicken
and apple pie
the smells of your kitchen
your smells, your sweat, your scent
keeps bringing me back

Writing the Memoir

Shelly Clark Geiser

Start naming names,
promote a walking tour
through a town full of ghosts.
Load up bedraggled, exhausted families:
mothers, brothers, aunts and uncles,
drive them to the country,
dump them onto a dusty road
under the noon-white sun.
Pull their pants down around their ankles.
Keep stripping layers: bat, belt, finger, zipper,
this is where the old sick father comes in
and the alcoholic brother, his trembling hands.
Next, a complete chapter for the mental-breakdown mother,
tweezing every hair from her head until it resembles
the naked light bulb above the bathroom sink.
Shave off the coarse black hair on your boyfriend's belly,
the boyfriend who is in love with himself.
Do it while he is sleeping.
Expose the kooky astrologer,
her psychic hot line single-handedly
keeping the lonely alive.
Dig deeper now,
there's probably an abortion somewhere
and institutional therapy.
Finally, in the climactic last chapter
take care of what's left:
the tattoos, the scars, the self-inflicted burns.
Now, the audience is in a frenzy, cheering in pain—
go ahead, eat all the way to naked bone,
slash every reachable vein.

Surely

Marilyn Coffey

And surely no silence exceeds the silence that lies unbroken
after countless hours of incessant wind
after endless days of wind that rags relentless
from Rocky Mountains to Mississippi
wind that wound pioneer mothers into shrieking tops
careening from wall to wall inside soddy huts
wind that never pauses to rattle weather vane to catch breath

                    Surely

                    no
                    silence
                    exceeds
                    this
                    silence

                    that
                    lies
                    now
                    unbroken
                    but
                    for

          the mosquito's piercing drone

          the cricket's bleat

          the fierce detonation
          of a June bug shell against
          my window screen.

Badlands Midnight

Marilyn Coffey

I stumble from my tent, swoon

No sky ever hung so utter black
no glitter of stars so lucid

Billions radiate a band so thick
I drop my jaw
to catch its cool Milky drink

At such an hour was I born:
squirming pink & brown & soft
into this black velvet world
ablaze with brilliants

With good reason I howled
my blood-red cry
held my eyes asquint
against this two-toned world
so possible, so impossible
so close-at-hand, so distant
eternal yet transient

vaporized by any other light:
the sun, street lamps
this match I light, lift
before my eyes:

This night mine
to annihilate
but not, I note
mine to summon

What Edie Sedgwick Taught Me about Success

Erin Croy

Freight elevator gate slams shut
the last time. My arms are full
of boxes.

You cannot die back east
no matter how much you stuff drugs
into the crook of your elbow,
or forty Benadryl and beer and whatever
pill he pressed into your hand,
amused. Crashing

a Mercedes in the city,
or a Korean car into a semi
won't do. Either of us can try
burning down the Hotel Chelsea,
but we'll wake, hands still wrapped in gauze,
or at least still

nauseated. Remember what you hoped
when you first rode the elevator up? Too bad
wild-haired boys in dark glasses
only give the time of day for a little while
and leave with ideas.
Go home, put on
a dress and marry
a simple man who picks you up
from shock treatment. Take the right
pills, only as prescribed and it will happen
like an accident.

The sun is only out
to set. My father is in the truck.
I am headed west
to be respectable.

Pigeons
Erin Croy

Outside on a smoke break—
there are doves
and pigeons on the roof of a church. I wonder
whether people drive by and think
I am a prostitute.
I am wearing worn-out
leopard-print flats with pointed toes.

I smoke, though
my lungs hurt. I wonder could it be
lung cancer at twenty-six. I am dying.
I am allergic
to the girl I work with upstairs.

I always try to explain
doves and pigeons are the same
bird. Doves are pigeons
with albinism, light
and acceptable. It's like angels
and homeless alcoholics.

I have an apartment. I could be
a drunk bum. It is not a tragedy
when a serious woman
dies. She escapes,
dark and dirt.

Back upstairs, the girl I am allergic to, me-
at-twenty-one, and I discuss
our fear of scales after
I weigh myself in a backroom
with a switchboard that smells like fish.
I want to say

It will be all right, but stupid
and not alcoholic and with
a husband and a son,
she is a dove.

I have a bruise
on the back of my left hand.

The Untidy Season

Same Spring

Erin Croy

It's been the same season
going on four years
now. It starts
to smell like new grass,
mud, and the Missouri
river. Out come
the sundresses
with breezy skirts, eighths
of weed we'll sell our plasma for
if we don't have
the money, long
daylight and boy-
watching on the front
cement steps with the dog
tied to the railing.

This year, one of us
is calm, and no one
will try to die.
We'll be content
with holes wearing
in the grass-stained knees
of last fall's jeans, forty-
ounce beers, and
waiting for the first
lightning bug.

Attachment

Cat Dixon

If one catches a splinter
while hammering a canvas
into a frame, he should not
dig with tweezers at the fleck
thus tearing at his flesh
like a melodramatic griever.
Instead, he should
let it be stuck under
the skin, a reminder
of the chore, of the woman
in the painting.
The epidermis has a mind—
knows when it's hurt,
when it's cold, alone.
It will rid itself of what
it needs to soon
enough. The sliver
will free itself
without notice until
he sits down to write
a letter, takes up a pen,
and sees it's finally gone.

Sunday Afternoon at Mission Park

Cat Dixon

My son and I survey the trees,
novice birdwatchers, to listen for chirps.
Instead of climbing on the play equipment
or sliding down the blue slide,
Pierce collects sticks that litter
the woodchips from last week's
storm. He, the preschool-sized
groundskeeper, hauls the pile
to the trash can and heads
to retrieve more debris.
Overhead the serenade starts again:
Pierce, Pierce, Pierce, Pierce, Pierce.

To find the bird, to know its name,
I want to climb the tree, to ascend
to the highest branch so I can write
about this bird that whistles
my son's name so clearly, and Pierce,
his arms akimbo, his brow scrunched,
smirks and asks,
Why that bird say my name?
It calls over and over, a joyful peck,
a canticle to a tiny god.

Tabula Rasa

Cat Dixon

From behind one-way glass,
I stare. The line-up
comprises him and him
and several more.
I point to each and each
is called forth—
come straight, turn to the side,
move to the back wall.

When asked who did it,
I say everyone.

The men sent to cells, the officers
go home, a janitor
sweeps by with a broom,
so I tap the glass,
call over the mike
to the narrow, empty tomb.

River

Cat Dixon

Weeks ago when the city's sewage operators dumped shit into the Missouri, people were warned not to swim, boat or fish in the water, yet there was a white boat out there, always one guy who didn't see the newscast or who just didn't give a fuck, on his 30-foot cruiser, blared music, wasting his batteries and letting his five-year-old aboard without a life jacket. That time. Weeks ago when the river was just a giant's toilet, a corroded pipe to the ocean, I needed to sit on the bank then. I did. My gray SUV's back hatch open wide like a yawn, my legs hanging from the bumper. There I sat. I drank Smirnoff straight. It tasted gray—the only color I can taste and feel, smooth as a flower's petals before they grow brittle. I drank amaretto—my baby's breath after she suckled. The wind blew; water rippled the stars. Drunk and nauseated from the smell, the chiggers bit me, the fireflies were candles to light my way, the mosquitoes drew my blood, took samples of it to some insect lab where every test came back positive or every test I failed, I strolled by the river's edge. I can't swim. Wading in, my brown flip-flops slipped off, my shirt and jeans weighed me down, my rocks. I can't back-float. I almost drowned in eighth grade. How disappointed I was with my savior, a bigger girl named Kay, who scooped me up as if I were a penny in a fountain. She had retrieved my wish so she could throw in her own, but that was Beaver Lake, this is the Missouri. I'll trudge forward into the current. The toilet will flush. My vomit, the night before, was silt-colored and I stared at it for hours. There, in my bathroom, I saw the bottom of the river. Everything that is too heavy to carry on, rests.

A Sandhills' Meditation
After Job

Mary Marie Dixon

Naked I came from my mother's womb.

Rose-cracked lips, scaley,
Suckling heat, pink polka dots
Wet under my breasts.

Naked I will return again.

Dust devils chafe skin
And bury kernels of threshed
Grain lost in hoofprints.

The Lord giveth.

A widened loop snares
A bucking limb, rope that burns
Paths in my greased hands.

The Lord taketh away.

The corralled herd breaks;
Barbed wire snaps snake venom
Into denim skin.

Blessed be the name of the Lord.

Who stables the stars,
Spurs the warring clouds to rain,
Rides the grassy tides?

And these are but the outer fringe of his works;
How faint the whisper we hear of him!

Who fences black birds,
Digs in the posts of heaven;
Who dams up the sky?

Sonnet on Craving

Eve Donlan

Pregnant, I'd acquiesce to the demand
Of my body, trusting its sharp hunger
Had wisdom of its own. To boiled eggs and
Potatoes in mayo I'd surrender,
Meeting needs I didn't know I had yet.
Less wholesome desires, though, I'll try to fight,
Like the draw of smoking "just one" cigarette.
Each cell and nerve is hounding me to light
Up, promising relief if I submit
And torment if I don't. But when both right
And wrong taste good, I'm not sure, I admit,
Whether the pangs are healthy appetite
Or addictive habit. Which one are you?
The urge I should resist—or give in to?

Moon of the Buffalo Coming

Marilyn Dorf

She asked when would the buffalo
come, and he said they wait
for the moon to carry their shadow.
Hunger Moon is best, he said,
that or the Grass Moon of April,
said how you wait until thunder
leaps off the far hill so you feel it
beneath you, rumbling your shoes,
loosening your bones, black shadows
leading them onward in thunder and dust,
their eyes white as almonds and barely
cracked open, hooves casting the world
lopsided under their weight. She said
that was enough, opened the door,
and said she'd ride off on one
of the other moons—the Crow Moon
or the Moon of the Full Long Nights.

Bullying

Lorraine Duggin

Nobody shouted, "Bully!" when Richard Hardy
crept up stairways early, sneaked into the 7th grade classroom
on the second floor where Sandy Stefanek sat eating her peanut butter
sandwich and apple from a brown paper bag. Sandy couldn't go home
at noon from Brown Park School like the rest of us
on a one-hour lunch break, her skinny legs braced
in steel, a wheelchair her main mobility after polio two summers ago,
though she could take a few slow steps, one at a time
with metal crutches up to her waist.

When Richard somehow evaded all the teachers who stayed
mostly in the library that hour, or the janitor, who stayed mostly
in the basement all the time, or the safety patrol kids, who wouldn't
come on duty until 20 minutes before the bell, he clutched a live sparrow
in his hand, little bird's heart beating as fast as a hummingbird's,
as rapidly as Sandy's a few minutes later when Richard Hardy's
menacing, hulking frame darkened the classroom doorway, confronted
Sandy alone with her lunch bag, forced her up from the desk,
horrified, her back precariously against the wall, gripping crutches,
world map in the corner, pushed her against the blackboard,
too dazed to scream, too shocked to do anything
but cling to crutches for dear life, trembling, moaning.

Though later when she told Mrs. Gamer, our teacher,
about the ghastly incident, and then the principal, Miss Reynolds,
who sent her home, Sandy sobbed and sobbed, curly blond
      hair mussed, damp
around her wet face, pale, blotchy with trauma, and then told
her best friend, Sharon, who told everyone and who accompanied
Sandy home to stay for the rest of the day
after Sandy's mother arrived in the car,

told how Richard, clutching the tiny brown sparrow,
thrust it in front of Sandy's teary, terrified eyes,
strangling the frantic, wildly chirping bird, decapitating it

with only the strength of his powerful hands inches from her face,
twisted off stringy veins and tangled knot of cords, bloody cartilage
of lifeless body in one hand, crushed sightless eyes,
matted feathered head all that was left in the other.

We all thought Richard Hardy, though I'm sure he was disciplined,
doomed for sure to annals of serial killers, rapists, psychopaths.
We all thought it just a matter of time before he'd end
his days behind bars, hanging from the gallows, or fried
in the electric chair, evil, frowning face making the front page.

But nobody at our last class reunion knew where he was now
or whatever happened to him. Someone thought he'd married
young, a plain girl from a different neighborhood, had kids,
sold insurance for a living. Another thought he'd dropped
out, remembered he didn't graduate with us. Someone else
could have sworn he'd joined the Marines, got shipped
someplace overseas, got the killing out of his system.

Avis

Deirdre Evans

Avis, you're gone.
You're gone and all your stories,
stretched over the phonelines
from Houston to Omaha,
like the sheets and pillowcases you ironed
to kill the nits,
are wadded up wrinkled in my uncertain memory.
You and I had no children
(the tumor you carried, then aborted from your womb,
implanted its offspring in your kidneys instead).

So who will listen now to your memories
of night soil emptied from thunder mugs, and
stubborn soot scrubbed from kerosene lamps;
such chores unknown to children who flip a light switch
and flush a toilet without a thought.

You hadn't minded, it was what poor folk did.
And everyone was poor, so you didn't mind that either.
You roamed freely through fields of blue bonnet wildflowers
and swam in clear, unpolluted streams.

What's it like, Avis? You said you were tired, ready to go.
I'm not that tired, you know? I still wake up with a to-do list,
curious to read the paper and wonder what happens next.
But now you know whatever it is we know next.
Is it nothing or are the fields of wildflowers,
gone for Texas highways, still fragrant in heaven?

You said not to be sad when you died,
but I notice the phone crouches despondently on the counter,
embarrassed to be so useless. I pop the champagne bottle's cork
to celebrate, since you said you thought it would be a rebirth.
You said if it turns out to just be nothing, that would be okay, too.

"Call me again, soon!" you told me a week ago.
I was busy and thought there would be more time,
stretching hazily ahead of me like that unending Texas highway.
You've gone to some state bigger than Texas
and I'm still here in Omaha consoling the phone.

The Untidy Season

December Morning Commute

Sarah Fairchild

White-flocked trees line Normal Boulevard.
The very air shimmers with glistening ice.
Everything seems soft and in slow motion.
Even the car accidents are beautiful:
Puffy marshmallows nudging
into each other in a slow dance,
muted red and yellow lights blinking
like the memory of Christmas trees,
skid marks and footprints gently
filling in with powdery snow.

Mars and Venus

Jackie Fox

Listen carefully, boys and girls
because what I am about to tell you
is the true difference between men and women.
Forget the *Book of How We're All Like Planets*,
the *Book of What I Heard and What You Meant*.
Make haste to the temple of gentlemen,
see the reverence in their upturned faces
while they worship at the altar of female flesh.
The only sound the pulsating music
as the dancers swirl like eddies
in a sea of desire, which parts each time
they open their lush thighs.
The men sit hushed
in this cathedral of longing,
made humble by the presence
of divine breast and arching back,
that grail of want and ache since time
began. Now hurry on down
to the Chippendales revival.
No silent veneration here.
The rowdy women whoop and stomp
as the men grind those glorious hips,
wave their dollar bills like flags
and leap into the aisle
as though drawn by the heady tug of Jesus
to the front of a tent, where
they will testify in the name of all that's holy—
of being gripped by the spirit
that calls forth their ecstatic moans,
pulls their throats skyward,
and commands the almighty shudder
to roll through them like a wave.

Surgeon

Jackie Fox

Those long, sure hands.
Holding yours in pre-op,
spreading calm like a drug.
Wiping blood from your hand
that the nurse missed on IV prep.
When she turns from the tray, says
in a voice like a blade edge,
"I can do that,"
he responds, "We're fine."
You know this is nothing more
than comfort; certainly
nothing less. And yet
you are a moth to a flame,
a moon to a planet,
a breast to the knife.

For Heidi Who Hates to Read in Public
And Asks Me My Secret

Monica Fuglei

To stop the quaking and shaking,
I think simply of a poet I know
who raises poems, children and pigeons.
For them he cleans the coops,
hand-feeding each, he stoops over their youth
and watches as they go, grow, and discover
the world.

At nearly a quarter of a century,
I am still quite young.

I know little of poems
and less of pigeons and children,
but when I see him,
I see them: children, pigeons, poems
and he watches, studies, loves them
as they lift off in purposeful flights
and return, always, return.

Fenced In

Kara Gall

These hips, rogue cattle:
the way pain catches
like a yoke on barbed wire
fence, the horns of a joint
trapped like some synovial fur
rubbed off on a metal spine
such a small thing, double-strand
twelve-and-a-half-gauge Red Brand
wire stacked on prairie clef
    such space between the lines
ilium and sacrum
bones believing
they might breach
the boundary of motion

Still Birth

Kara Gall

First-calf heifers require a hand
from time to time, or a whole arm
as the case may be, my husband
sheathed to shoulder in clear plastic
disposable gloves, feeling for
fetlocks, hitching and looping chains.
He is more now than just mere man
arms-length deep inside a warm cow
as he navigates the dark wet
geometry of birth, coaxing
the calf to dive out right-side-up,
head and front feet first.

A small contracted moan, tender
like a sigh, slips past the flat-topped
teeth of this young Herford mother,
my husband behind her, pulling
one calf leg at a time, the rolled
edges of his shirt unfurling
onto his bloody biceps. He frowns,
concentration dragging at his
mouth, sly tease of torque and tension.

              I squat next
to the figure of my firstborn,
having promised him a backstage
pass to this show, *the miracle
of life*, playing season after
calving season in the dusky
splintered shadows of a barn stage.
My husband calls me city when
I say it this way, but I was
born, raised, married, bred, and will die
cranking the handle of karmic
mysteries just as grandmother
fed corn through the shelling machine.

So it should not have surprised me
as it did when the calf slid free
to this world having already
departed for the next. We stood,
my son and I, our unborn awe
sticky in our hands, the mucous
slap of a cattleman pounding
against the stiff wet lungs of death,
the low bellow of a mother
acknowledging what she had known
four hours earlier in a pasture
hollow. Then she is silent, black
eyes unblinking behind the chute.

My husband is all joints and boots
kneeling hard angled into straw
littered floor, one hand to his head,
the other staining red his chaps
as his fingers reach a prayer
toward the calf's black form. My son asks
Why isn't he getting up now?

I wonder—*Do you mean daddy
or the calf?* Each death like the first,
like food that finds no mouth
like a horse with broken leg
like the flood washes away road
like hail upon a field of wheat
or a roof torn by tornado.

I wanted this birth like the first,
like the ancients sang up the sun,
giggling, maybe, at their foolish
fear that this would be the one year
it did not return. It never
crossed my mind to warn my son—
          never crossed my mother's to warn me—
that some things are born already
dead, that a star might rise too close
to earth and in its char black dawn
torch us all.

Writer's Block

Kara Gall

Last winter, the blizzards like bookends sat
for five months upon an empty shelf, not
a single sheet of paper where you hoped
there would be tomes—or at least paragraphs.

Wait for a seed, wait for the Beltane fires.
You yearn to burn these pointless blocks of wood,
to stir the ash with water into ink.
For now, content your hands with dusting shelves

your faded rag dragged across the fine-closed grain
polishing the knotted walnut plank,
a yogi humming breath into each pose.
Each breath out, the winter freeze. Each breath in,

you birth the burning solstice sun. Crackling
tiny hairs of dusty insight prickle,
antenna on the skin of unformed words.
It sneaks up under the surface of things,

gradually splitting the silty smooth earth
softening the hard seed coat, snapping
life open like a Little Bluestem shoot promises
to blaze across cold pasture.

From the sandhill dunes and mixed grass prairie,
atop the loess hills and stark eroded
canyons, the hard-fisted language finds you.
A poem eats only the meat it hunts,

freezing your apathy until snow melts,
thawing all your weakness until words, like
a writhing clutch of water, hatch beneath
the winter ice, slithering toward the spring.

Weather

Megan Gannon

What the rain erases
from a safe distance isn't

worth mentioning. Dishes
rinsed and dripping, still

door on its hinges, glass
tightening in panes.

This isn't accusation; it's only
we keep wanting beyond

all breadth and sense.
A woman stands by bare

windows, outside whitening
under the steady fall of her

attention. Even memory,
that ticking, how-long-gone

longing erases the direction
of weather. Even waking.

If we have souls we want them
to look like this: ground,

and not-quite-sky and light.

Dungeness
Cumberland Island, Georgia

Megan Gannon

Terraces, alcoves along the pergola
where a cocktail is set down, left,

early-summer shoreward showers
chiming like knives. A toast:

to the Carnegies; to names
that carry with them the sound

of well-mannered music;
to socialites tottering beside fountains,

to fountains flinging like flowergirls;
to twittering abandon that catches

in branches like the tossed-off
veils of pirate brides; to the dark

parts of the property where
electric lights don't reach;

to late-night, to servants
sweating their white gloves;

to histories easily erased, tabby
mortared from the shell-heaps

of long-gone tribes; to the names
scoured from gravestones

by salt wind and dangled
from trees like mermaid tresses;

to rumor; to underpaid-workers-turned-
arsonists; to ivy softening what

wouldn't burn—all the concrete
window sockets, the falling walls;

to ghosts that don't linger
in rooms that need weeding;

to thoroughbreds loosed on a wilding
island, manes tattered as the trees.

The Dead, Dreaming

Megan Gannon

In this half-gleam
we don't
    sleep, but glisten

continuously.
    Where the light
might—
    we catch, sheet

lifted and bit
in the pin.

Does it concern you, this
being of one body?
    Consider

hair, how much of it
is wind, how the wind
    tatters

to tendrils and the tendrils
touch.
    To be inside such

opalescence,

skin of milkglass, with inmost
listening the bridge of evening
and a child's lost progress
    past us

disquiets.

Dreaming, her one foot
leaving, we cling.

We would air her
    nothingness

among us, safe
  from the brightness,
    the pulsing,

and the pocket of eggs
seed deep in our teeth.

Daphne Digging In

Megan Gannon

Tarnish-scent
of times
    skin
felt tight
and touch-shy,
    the many
buds of my body ready

        to break
under hot breath.

Rustling, heat-steeping—

this movement always
outward

    so slow
it can't be seen.

I could be swift as riverwater
or still as ground,
    and yet the feeling

that all my daily turnings
were toward a center

      I could not cull,
deeper into a self and a shell
I'd always felt but not felt flesh.

Pliant in the never-still,
susurrus as a mind that stirs

spent wings. How climbingly
the heartwood fills.

Can silence
be heard inside
    such swayings,
rapturous from a root? Bright,

a high singing in extremities,
taking me elastic,

    weightless,
wider, the clearest

    chartreuse
rinsing like a gaze.

Mayday

Gaynell Gavin

> *And there was war in heaven: Michael and his angels*
> *fought against the dragon. ...*   Rev. 12

How your mother and aunt were there—your
hair was dark like theirs—we were young, our
children younger, our child support didn't come
that month or most others, the outside plaza air
soft as our late-afternoon caramel sundaes
—your favorite—life so sweet I thought
none of you would ever leave me. Oh, Michele,
fighting holy wars, how I miss you most in May.

Training

Karen Gettert Shoemaker

Like my mother,
I palm cradle
the yellow stick
of butter
like a giant crayon,
press its melt
into the crust
of fresh-baked bread.

Time folds in on itself
and on this kitchen so many miles,
oh god,
so many miles
from home.

The egg noodles
in the bubbling soup—
store bought.

If I close my eyes
I can recall
the rhythm of the rolling.
Thick dough thinning
to her nod.

But who has time for all that now?

We will be sated. We will believe
this good. This meal I make
instead of poems, or money.

More than once she told me she wanted
never to cook again. But cook she did
until there was no one at her table,
not even her own hunger.

Hungry

Karen Gettert Shoemaker

We cook over the fire
our yearning builds.

Start with a massive bundle
Of Hurt by Your Silence twigs,
a long branch from the Tree of
You Don't Listen to Me—well-soaked
in the kerosene of hidden tears.

We are experts at our craft.

Don't stop to admire
the crackle of it yet. Here's
the log of Waiting
to be Understood, a limb
of Half-Remembered Slights.

We are just getting started.

Here you come now
with a truckload of comebacks
you've been saving
for just this occasion. Soft
cottonwood from the I Trusted You Grove
goes in first. Then you stand
on the pile and use both hands,
to throw oaken chunks of
You Are Not My Mother
one after another into the flames.
I stoke the pyre with the red-hot poker of resentment.
Together we build an inferno that scrapes night from the sky.
Sparks pop and scatter in brimstone-inspired glee
until one catches my skirt.

Here we are.

Both of us smolder now.
Forced by instinct or habit
you save me. Supper
will be late again.

In the Far Field
after The Hailstorm *by Thomas Hart Benton*

Crystal S. Gibbins

clouds orchestrate their mischief,
with some secret agenda,
susurrus wind, and blood stroke
of lightning, sweeping away
the rooted, the untethered,
bending blue grass, withering
the strength of brick buildings.
A mere drizzle is no tragedy.
The ground surrenders to the armada
of hail, the field sprawls and twists;
stones swell; leaves fall earthward
toward their next cycle, nuzzling
into loam, erasing themselves
into humus. And the sower slogs
through his chores slow-dancing
to sky's brute turn that drones
the same saturated phrase,
in the same cadence again and again
like a lost airplane, a crop duster,
still circling. He tries to count
each collapsed stalk of corn,
each petrified clump of grass,
but loses track too fast to know
where he started, learns quickly
that these days, these hours,
these places are all about counting.
He wonders how many sins are worn
down by how many storms? How many
layers, how many stones and bones,
just how much dirt? The possibilities,
the dimensions, I'm sure won't add up,
but there is not much else for him to do
in this wide open they call the heart-
land, this place in the middle
mid-drift, absolute middle,
the mid-land of nothing
but land, flat canvas to paint.

Signs

Crystal S. Gibbins

Last night I made dinner
again without complaint,
only silent brooding over
boiling potatoes and leeks—
their roots no longer reaching
into mud. You stood
at the edge of the kitchen
tiles, watching me stir
the spoon against the kettle;
my hands slow in their circular
signature, agreeing to the loss
of what dissolves—
the potato's sugar and bits
of leaf. But you didn't know
I craved the heat of cayenne
in the back of my throat;
and when I called you over,
you sat on one side of the table
and I on the other.
We didn't speak.
You kept busy, feeding.
How seemingly simple:
when hungry, eat;
when tired, sleep.
I lifted my eyes and pushed
my bowl across the table.

Nebraska Highway 15 on an April Day

Jane Goossen Wolfe

Traveling north on Nebraska 15,
I anticipate the highway
seams which rattle my spine.

Last winter snow clung
to fence lines like the plaque
building inside my father's head.

Today I brake for wild turkeys
and watch a bluebird carry
grass to a nesting box.

As I drive toward Dad and
his newly cracked bones,
dust blows across the highway.

Dry cornhusks spiral near the
old farmhouse whose splintered
porch sags toward the ground.

Sunday Morning

Jane Goossen Wolfe

Alone in my house, I breathe in
steam from the mug of tea
warming my palms. Young birch
leaves flutter in the soft Spring
sunrise. If I were surrounded by
bluegrass, I'd listen for the whisk
of my grandmother's broom.
Just under a distant ridge, I'd
sit in a hollow, where damp
ground cradles my pelvis
and the wind rocks me home.

Here, Now

Teri Grimm

I've seen you walk into familiar rooms as though you'd wandered
into a strange forest at night. Cold and bewildered, you've forgotten
how to be hungry. I hold you and it's like hugging a small tree in winter.
Stiff branches are your arms. Brittle twigs your fingers.
Tremors rise through your body
because the earth shifts beneath you.
Tremors rise through your body
because something large is lumbering toward you.
I don't want the ground to swallow you up.
I don't want the shadow to steal you away. Mama,
I hold you so you can protect me from these things.

I See Men as Trees Walking

Teri Grimm

Mark 8:24

That one is Willow, thin and prone
to bend any way the wind blows

strong. He is friends with that one,
Poplar, who stays also near the river.

His kind grows up fast, though not well
favoring drink as they do. Cypress

lives nearby, but will not be warped.
That one loses all his leaves and is ashamed

winter long. That one loses all his leaves
and is never ashamed though should be.

Fir stays lush through cold and screens
righteousness and evil without passing

judgment. Over there, a family called Figs yield fruit
sweet and good, though some do not. They are

considered warned. Oak stands on a hilltop
looking down on all that happens

beneath, yet ignores the pests
devouring his own heart. Dark as it is

outside and hard, pests don't bother Acacia
holding fast like Pharisees, the letter of the law,

but not the spirit. Rich and wicked is
Bay. Covetous and showy is Palm.

Olive is the source of feuds and Cedar
will be sacrificed. Pomegranate's

alluring and bears beautiful fruit.
Her skin is tough, her flesh is full

of seeds and she knows
she was not worth the trouble.

Near the Platte

Twyla Hansen

On a wooded trail
the small waterfall is half frozen,
half emptying its bucket
over the edge of ancient plate rock,
the exposed formation in hills
that ancient people roamed,
gathering sticks and branches fallen
for their communal fire,
their luck of bounty and nomadic ritual.
Standing near it, we breathe snowmelt
and slight breeze, while overhead
the sun hides behind a layer of cloud.
We've had more than our share
this winter, we complain.
When will it ever end, we ask.
Later, back at the cabin,
we clink glasses, toast
the soreness of muscles, the red
of cheeks, the rip and roar
of logs now all warmth and flame.
The fact that we are here, alone
together, liquid flowing
freely from bottle and tap,
our ritual gathering and communion
homage to those before us, nomad
and immigrant and parent, lucky, our
lives blessed, eyes filling with smoke.

Omens

Allison Adele Hedge Coke

Here, owl swooped down from roof edge
over night bearing dawn under closed lid
heavy with rest. Messenger immemorial.

We awake this way, reaching over swells
cresting undercurrents, news from before, now,
knowing sleep brings wisdom, three lids full.

He turns toward us, momentarily. Shoots
away into gnophos, kimririm, qadhruth,
as the 6:07 coal cars churn beginnings of light.

May we harbor whatever moves us
in wing-scooped still, to the edge here,
toss it underneath rail steel, return to sleep, sleep—

Summer 1996

Carolyn Helmberger

When it rained in Dublin,
I expected earthworms
on the sidewalk. Instead,
it was sprinkled
with snails. Careful not
to crunch them, I hop-scotched
over those tiny fossilized
cinnamon rolls on our
playground, Trinity
College. Under the D.A.R.T.
tracks I counted them, surprised
to see so many struggling along,
slugs carrying their means
on their pliant bodies.
Sixty-five soaked
up the Irish rain, the first drops
stamping the sidewalk with
dark grey kisses, smacking
their lips against the concrete.
When we walked home
from the pub, the snails
dissolved somewhere
into the heedless rain
and we abandoned the night,
closing your red door behind us.

Anniversary #23, No Sex for Me

Fran Higgins

I wrote the evening, planned
    the details down.
        They fell—the details, the evening—
as the muscle seized and locked my stance
    in bent agony.
Erotic celebration out of the question,
    to straighten, merely, would be a joy.

The deep-red, silk roses, from their vase,
    mock my imperfection
        with their sensual petals,
            their upright stems.

Fanam's Car Repair & Tow

Fran Higgins

Drunk teens supply a steady stream
of business to the lot. Carlos, Laurie,
Roger aimed to beat a train but ended
up in pieces on the track. Fanam
towed the twisted metal back, but locked
it in a shed—too gruesome for display.
The metal skeleton of a charred truck
whose driver burned to death, fingers welded
to the wheel when a locomotive struck,
reposes on the lot beside a car
that flipped on highway 80 west
of town. Crushed with windows broken all
around, a child's single shoe waits on
the seat. A piece of lettuce stained with blood
wilts on the armrest in the sun.

Sisters in a Cistern

Samantha Hubbard

Bronchitis burns our throats
As the soap did when mother
Washed our mouths out
For taking the Lord's Name in vain
    As if
Her Brillo-pad nails could scrub us free
Of our transgressions.

We spend weeks
Drinking well water,
And eating teaspoons
Of Neapolitan quarts.
We convalesce long past
Our diagnosed affliction:
We like our skinny selves.
Covered by a crazy quilt,
We laze on a feather-tick mattress,
Play UNO and honeymoon bridge,
Watch Oliver North's defense
On a 13-inch screen,
Eat less
And
Less.

Your last night, we float
Like cottonwood seeds,
Come to rest on the west lawn,
And watch the sun set.
Our own palms' touch
Scrubs us free
As the corn dust blends
Burnt orange to blackened blue.

From the Farm Yard

Samantha Hubbard

I watch your outline in the combine cab
as you harvest the Star Place,
the quarter you share-cropped in the 50s.
The sky turns olive drab;
you rock the seat,
urge the beast
faster.

On evaporated puddles
my bare feet crunch clumps
that look like pine cones.
Mares whinny and buck,
flip manes and tails,
follow the sorrel stallion
who rears and knocks down a fence post.
The hail barbs fall.

Three days later,
the graders smooth ruts in the road
while we fix
fence.
Your forearms sinewy, strong, work
the post-hole digger.
When you strike rock,
son-of-a-bitch,
you yell for the rock,
the horses, the hail,
the place
measured for you.

The Almost Man

Joy Von Ill

bites into a plum.
Juice slips into his beard,
his feet dig at the plush carpet.

His eyelids almost touch me,
a book falls off the table,
a golden shepherd on the cover.
My hand grasps the table leg.

He almost falls off the floor,
the curtain stays still.
The blinds tell us to move.

I almost lay my head in his lap,
saying, "I own a tent peg.
Are you my enemy?"
A chest hair falls on my face.
My lungs rise.

He almost finds the pattern
in the ceiling tiles,
and I find the pattern in
ignoring his breaths.

I almost
    want
        a bite of plum.

I lean over the slanted couch,
drop a penny on a string, to find
the straight line.

My pink nail almost scrapes
the back of his knee,
tendons and muscles uncovered.

He almost touches my hip
bone—pushing flesh aside,
Like old rotten leaves.
I give him back his rib,
whispering, "I didn't really want this."

He Dreamed My Bed Was a Sandbox

Natasha Kessler

He dreamed my bed was a sandbox
where he built a castle.
In the castle, he hid a shell.

When we reach our hands
deep inside—
so deep they fall into the ocean—
we find a pair of mittens

he said were for winter
and a soft crab's shell.

I'd like to slip
inside its cool mouth.

If he had the power
to force-feed seagulls,
he'd tell you stories about their faces—
the way they look when they can't swallow.

When we wake in the morning,
I want you to tell stories like that.

How to Read a Small-Town Newspaper

Maureen Kingston

Out of respect, start with pages two and three: the obits on the left, newborns on the right, anniversaries near the middle fold.

Then flip to the back page, to the smaller-fonted court news: divorce decrees, property transfers, minors in possession of god-knows-what, the out-of-town speed demons, the credit card deadbeats.

Next, spy the photos: the mayor's hands in every picture, passing out plaques and over-sized checks, waving the parade in; and note the action shots of legalized violence: spiked volleyballs, half-nelsons, chop blocks.

Ignore *all* the minutes—library board, school board, city council— dullards without their executive sessions attached.

Back to the front page for clarification and official versions of the day's gossip already chewed: the tractor rollover crushed his arm *not* his leg; the sidewalk improvements *will* require a penny tax; and nobody's drawers dropped during the senior center fashion show (least-wise there's no art to settle the matter one way or the other).

A quick glance at the boxed items as needed: church service times for visitors; school lunch menus for parents (kids don't appreciate wieners and beans two meals in a row); the map for this weekend's town-wide garage sale.

And, finally, read the opinion page: left, right (mainly right), and center. All imported, of course.

Is This the Haircut of a Woman Rebuffed?

Ruth E. Kohtz

Staring down the evening against a lean wind
Wishing on stars for a car accident
Wishing on cars for a star accident

No luck—
night opens, and a mouth
tangles up wishes.

Dreams

Ruth E. Kohtz

At night, we sleep without touching
You have dreams directed by Quentin Tarantino and
I tumble through the million different ways I could lose you

In the morning you roll over, clutch hand to breast, to tell me where
    you've been:
shot-gunning PBR in an abandoned attic with Frank Zappa again
while I was at a giant Super Bowl bra-fitting where you were dating my
    best friend from 3rd grade

The next night you are one of a dozen henchmen, killing people and
    transporting their bodies,
screaming "No, man, we didn't get Tanya!"
While in my sleep I receive a psychic's death sentence so you take me to a
    cave of ice cream sculptures and promise—"If you had lived I would
    have married you"

At this, I kick for the surface, gulping daylight
having escaped both death and separation from you for the millionth
    time
I give you mouth to mouth so I can breathe,
scared of what my visions mean

You pause, while describing the hit-man dream,
to look into my eyes and ask me

"Do you think it's because I threw that frozen squirrel in the trash
    last night?"

Half-Cooled Coffee

Karma Larsen

a note to my daughter

it is my mother's hands I spread before me
dark, mottled, scarred
nails dirty from yesterday's weeding
it is her hesitance I feel with you
all the questions she never asked
and all the ones she did, the simple ones
a thread passed to me to hold onto
sometimes I didn't give the answer
but now I, too, long to pass this filament
to bind us together.

I remember my mother with her friend Emma
country and city lives, so little in common
grave and earnest at the round kitchen table
coffee cooling in their cups
though I didn't listen to their words
I understand now what bound them
the hard tales, the painful twists
children whose paths turned and turned again.

too late, I want to sit at table with them
with you
drink the half-cooled coffee
laugh a bit
enter, kindly, each other's sorrows

Five Young Men

Karma Larsen

> ...*You are not here to verify,*
> *Instruct yourself, or inform curiosity*
> *Or carry report. You are here to kneel*
> *Where prayer has been valid.*—T.S. Eliot

bits of the story keep seeping out
spots of bright red blood seeping under the door
how, as they entered the car
the one who yelled shotgun
sat instead in back, didn't know the roads as well
how the lights bearing down on them
were only visible for a mere second
then darkness
so that the liquid they felt
on their faces, their hands
had no color, only warmth.
i try to wrangle the words, the images
wrestle them into lines here on the page.
in hearing the story, telling it
it is so difficult to keep the young men straight
the names, the injuries
the fourth name gets left out in every telling
we stumble, pause, look away.
and how strangely for me the fifth young man
the one we did not know
the one in the pickup
continues to haunt
he too is someone's son.
and so we walk out into the world
enter our cars, raise our sons
and cry holy, holy, holy.

Prairie

Karma Larsen

…the end of all our exploring
Will be to arrive where we started
And know the place for the first time.—T.S. Eliot

Dreams are more insistent than thought.
Won't be ignored.
I had been in Paris one month, maybe two.
Night after night the same dream.
A train, fast-moving
the landscape outside almost a blur
but familiar, one I knew.
Flat land, waving grasses, blue sky
sunshine, prairie in all directions.
Inside the train I wanted only for it to stop
knowing it wouldn't.
Knowing soon I would be in a city
what city, what day, I didn't know
Paris, Munich, Venice.
But the land outside my window
where I wanted to go
slow down, step down, enter it
walk in the grass, alone,
as far as my feet would take me.

The Cranes

Karma Larsen

it was the spring of my father's cancer
week after week, the trip home
barren fields, winter skies
the end of those journeys palpable from the
beginning

and then, the gift
sandhill cranes arrived
form so simple
as if God, with His finger, had drawn two swift lines
more graceful than any before
the power of that form remembered
spring 1980, Beginning Drawing 101
(taken not so I could see what my hands would draw
but to see how the fields, the horizon
could be lifted, placed there on the canvas
to remind us where we came from)
on that day only a cold statue in a museum display
a sandhill crane, stiff, bereft of the real—
the fields, the sky—
my hands tried, but failed
then Jacobshagen beside me
taking the paper, the pencil,
attentive to the lifeless form before me
then back to my fingers, but the spell was broken
the bird stretched and lifted
abandoned the cramped display

Looking for Cancer

Karma Larsen

with thanks to Ted Kooser

Three years past
but it's habit by now
a way of looking at the world.
I look for it, find it
sometimes clear
sometimes parable
A dog on point, a bluebird
it's there later, at the side of the road
and in a hallway where a woman slowly lifts her foot.

It's like being in a room full of people
everything surface, dull, mundane
and then, across the room
a hand is lifted
or a word spoken
in a language not everyone speaks.
Suddenly it's there
a map
the way through
one traveler to another.

Revelation in Rapid City

Mary Logan

After three-hundred miles without a word,
you say I will be yours forever,
a ring burns in your pocket.
Now you wait for me, slouching and smoking,
flicking a branding iron out the window
of the rust-bucket Duster.

I watch a biker pull out of the rest stop
on a black and red shovel-head,
leathered face a worn saddle kept supple with oil.

He rides off alone, boots spurring highway pegs,
leaning back on a bedroll,
heading towards the Badlands,
on the next best thing to a roan Appaloosa.

You don't know I have already gone
without a word on a ghost-flamed Harley
to Medicine Bow to be no one's forever,
escaping the ring and the rope and the brand.

Antelope County Cemetery

Mary Logan

Lance-leaf cottonwoods stand here
where he lies,
across the road flat fields of brome,
the bluegill lake choking on moss
and storm-felled oaks.

Take away the formal flowers
carnations, roses, wax-lipped lilies,
snapdragons grown in a humid house.
Plant instead a bank of rue,
herb of grace for fallen stones.
Let bindweed, bitterbrush and nightshade grow.
Lay sweet William in the ground.

Dusk

Judy Lorenzen

The sleek cat of evening
leaps high on silent paws,
curling up the day,
filling this kitchen windowsill
with night.
One eye shut;
the other,
a slice of yellow-green moon,
peers in
drowsily.

A Sonnet for My Son
for Andrew Joseph Maasdam

Cathy Maasdam

Because I knew that you would be the last
child of my womb, I made a promise to
myself to linger, cherish, not let pass
a single moment's time alone with you.
And so, by moonlight we would meet, night after night,
the house unconscious, dark and still,
your tiny fingers wrapped around mine—so tight
a band of flesh on flesh held there until
you fell asleep. And then, though late the hour
I'd stay, one moment more, my arms your bed,
to languish in the touch, the taste, the flower
of baby's breath, to kiss your silken head.
My plan to make our moments last would fail—
time, so sacred, went rushing faster still.

Confession of Faith

Kelly Madigan

When I remembered how to pray
the elm branches had already developed their dark streaks.
The bruise of northern lights flared,
and the wind heaved the sides of my canvas tent.
How long had I been traveling? My sisters
had launched into the river years ago, and eggs cooled
in the nests. My arm ached from throwing rocks into the water,

and when queried, the prophet laughed with a choking sound
and picked glass from his feet. I remained on the bank
because of some way the water swirled, the intoxicating
effect of current. All day I would lie on an old mattress
and play melodies on my mouth organ. I needed to know

how so much water could be on the move and mute.
The bread I carried went blue with age, and my hair grew down
to the blades protruding from my back. All night
the elm bark beetles packed up illness,
bearing it like gifts to the next tree.

I'd like to say it happened in a factory,
at an ornate altar, in a rail car. I'd like to tell you
I came out of isolation to look at the faces of people,
to have them clasp my shoulders and tell me the news.

The truth is prayer came to me in a beetle,
with my ear pressed to the trunk, where the Lakota man
said there is a tinkling voice, a music being made
inside of old trees. Prayer stopped being a puzzle
and became a boat made of bark with a lantern swung over
the side. That is how I left the wide river. I am not writing this
down for you, I know already it cannot be replicated.
But when they say I did not believe,
point to the dazzle of light on the overside of leaves.
Open your hand and show them the beetle.

Muster

Kelly Madigan

My father stationed states away,
my father at Air War College.
My father on reel-to-reel tape.

My father's pressed blue uniforms.
Green zippered flight suit.

My father the navigator.
My father's dissertation
specifying the movement of tornadoes
across the Great Plains. My father
with shotguns, with lures, with leave.

My father TDY, on alert, my father
seeding clouds with dry ice. My father
deciphering ocean currents. My father

during the Cuban missile crisis, my father
at my crib. My father with elephants,
my father of six continents. My father
at Global Weather.

My child father escaping the landlord's
eviction, my father thin and pious. My father's
rote memory, his passive vocabulary. My father
and stocks, and driving lessons. My father
of the Scotch and water.

My father's replacement valves. My father stockpiling.
My father of favors, of payment. My father's
shoe shine kit, my father with a needle-nose pliers.
My father the colonel.

My father deliberating. My father's father
afraid of wind. My father's balcony.

My father's match head,
my father's ticks. My father with rheumatic
fever, my father's scarred heart.

My father
of languages, my father of Strategic
Air Command, of body surfing. My father
of peel-your-own shrimp, of templates.

My father's wild poems. My
father's quarters, his black wallet. My
father's blackmail, my father at the blackjack
table. My father superior, my father
weeping. My father's property. My father's limbs
and torso, my father on the gurney, my father's salute.

Power Outage on a Clouded Moonless Night
Kelly Madigan

Every lit thing now dark
at the center and the edges, no coil of hibernating
brightness that saved itself through torpor or feigned death.

The rectangle of valanced glass
now no different than the lathe and plaster
around it, the near and far away

equally obscured. The proverbial hand waving
before the face might as well be bats in remote caverns.
Dark moves against the shoulder of dark

as we have faith in, and attend to, the accretion
of other faculties, as we palm and tap,
eavesdrop, sample and sip the edge of known things.

He Leaves, She Stays

Kelly Madigan

There are snakes coiled in the toilet
tank, but I still remember security,
the smell in the house after food
had been slow cooked.

After I defended myself and was sure
I could not continue, you nailed thin
boards to hold the rotted ceiling in place.
Something greater came and loomed
above me, the musical light
of stars, and I was awake
for many days. When the sirens sounded
we did not take shelter, love,
we went out to the dark yard
to stare at the spin cloud.

It's over. I am smashing the last glass
in the white sink. If you were here I'd yell
something fortuitous. If you
need me, I'll be in a cave
made by throwing our bedclothes
over the tabletop, I'll be in there
reading Rumi to the dog
until the end days. You are still
welcome here, though you are
always silvered and whispering. My knees
have given in, and the dog cowers,
but these are your walls, your grace.
These are your dirty little walls.

Let's Pretend You're Touching Me

Ciara N. McCormack

but your finger is floating
                    millimeters

from the lines
            of my stomach

and *touch* is rather my skin rising,
        reaching and falling
                        in a wave
            that follows you gliding
along the elastic edge of my panties

And beyond that

I want to pretend you're kissing
            my neck

so when I close my eyes, every
                    tiny swirl

of your tongue
in the shadowed crevice
of my collarbone
becomes another turn of the room
            spinning on its own,
        expanding and blending
    into the universe.

—For S.

Laundry

Sheryl McCurdy

Though obscured by panes of cotton sheets
Harnessed between the ancient elms
I knew that silhouette
Mother hanging laundry in March winds
Head bent to the task
Mouth pursed about wooden clips

I did not help but hid and stared instead
Smelling the clean bleached day
Watching the billows of our bedding engulf her
Snapping and cracking like a whip

June, Maybe

Jean McDonough

I.

I want my mother back. And while I'm asking I
want all of my dead and missing pets
back, too. I want every cat that was hit by a car
and the baby mice found in the
garbage—their small pink bodies covered
with bits of lint and paper. And I want
my dog back, too. The one who was poisoned
who suffered on the cold floor
of the laundry room while I watched through a
rectangle of louvers because
my mother felt that death was something a
door should be between.

II.

Morning brings industry, a plume
of geese, yellow, the color of cowardice. I
am a griffin made of stone
and no emotion is the final one.
Nor is this the end
a rumble of panic, a reflection of sky
and the anguish of never looking up from a
list of things to do: post office, bank,
grocery store. Now, grief branches over
me, all time is local
and no objection is prohibited
by God.

We sat on the grass, the outline
of her recent grave still visible
because the sod had been newly placed—the

lines as apparent as a hem or a cut-line on a
Butterick pattern.
In the middle, an aluminum cylinder
waits for the flowers we brought:
lilacs and lily of the valley.
Sister, do you remember sitting on the edge
like that—the flowers a centerpiece, our mother
below? It was too soon for her marker
to have been placed—June
maybe.

Estate Sale

Deborah McGinn

We'll skip church for it,
forgive us.
Look, look at this fancy house,
a ranch style fifty decades long.
Girl brings a pot of pansies
to sit atop a yellow kitchen counter—
color and something living.
A hint of dog, Clorox, dark black coffee.
In my mind I am stripping wallpaper,
painting walls, ordering new wood floor,
fresh tile, ivory blinds, gold fixtures.
A man in bibby overalls yodels,
on his knees laying new carpet for the basement.
Blueprints in my head: widening windows
where the Christmas tree will go,
a new front porch with swing.
When the new appliances come I'll say,
over here. New stools and sinks
arrive I'll say, *in here* and *right there*
fifty different times.
House price tag down by $100,000.
I almost gulp at the price still affixed,
ducking in the bedroom with quilts
and linen suits, limp and dusty.
I bring home two Rockwell calendars
and a *Hello Dolly* album,
all for a dollar-fifty.

Tarcoles River

Cynthia McGowan

On route to Jaco, we pull over to the Tarcoles, over to where tourists lean up against barriers between them and the world. Over to where tourists pose, backs to the river, jape for their friends. *We're taking risks. This isn't home. There are crocodiles below!*

Frances lights up. On the horizon, more rain. We follow guardrail to the gap where some kids, or a kid, local kids, stole the tubing, the hole they leave yawning, where a kid, or some kid, a tourist kid, could slip through, where a drunk man could stumble, where the world could seep in, send a lone *gringo* gliding, zipline to silt bottom, hands flailing, grasp breasts of *la ninfa del rio*, give way to dim murk where the sun can't get through.

Crocodiles wait, inhaled breath, heat shimmer, as well-fed and smug as a nest of Republicans, bisecting nature, still air, stiller water. To move risks detection, the sunlight best hoarded.

Back in the car, we dodge potholes and mudslides, veer away from the street dogs, the car a slim barrier between us and the world. In Jaco, drenching rain empties streets, shops, restaurants, sends surfers, some surfers, surfboarders to hostels. We trudge on to the ocean, lean into the wind.

Leaning into the wind, waves rush out to greet us, dusk a flimsy barrier between us and the night. Sand sucks out beneath us, our feet flail for purchase, sand-bottomed lacunae where rivulets pool.

If you were here, I would wait, under water, eyes aglitter, never moving, hoarding secrets, my arms the sole barrier between you and the world. Bisecting your glance, clouds open on moonlight, clouds run like a river where nature seeps through.

At the Cancer Treatment Center

Jolene Moseman

I heard them giggling
inside the dressing room
after my mother went
in to help Dad
pull off his shirt and
tie the hospital gown shut.

He followed the nurse
to radiation
and left us with a wave,
his folded clothes
a few weeks
and white flecks of hair
on the inside rim of his cap.

A Plague of Sparrows

Maria Mullinaux

Because last year we gave them
the garage, slowly our house this
year is being consumed by sparrows.
They are invading the basement
from the crack they've widened
between the front steps and the
concrete wall that gives into
the pantry, and already they
have come from the eaves to
nest in the connecting airspace
and inside the second floor's
south walls. The airspace and
walls of the children's rooms.
And the children love cats, doves,
rodents, hawks, and sparrows.

Neither of the cats can sleep,
hysterical to scratch, to get
out on the roof. They do not
forget necessities. But you and I—

Near this window, hear them.
Behind the plaster. Eating.
Pecking. Playing two ends
against the middle
with the exact subterfuge
of small things against large,
go for the eyes and ankles,
ask father first, then mother
and the middle will fall down.

We can do nothing.
So small their bodies,
so clever their mock
broken wings,

and the brown tan white
black fragile colors
of their feathers,
and the hungry crying
dark to dark.

What bursts first
always the heart.

They will eat on and on
until the house
falls around us
and it is winter
and the cries
of our own children
startle us
awake
and hungry
while we let them feed.

Waiting It Out

Maria Mullinaux

In the full moon, Sirius is rising,
but not for that
do I stand half mad
between living room and stairs,
refusing to go up,
to listen to my son's
restlessness in sleep.
It would not help
any more than would recounting
the forces that have shaped him.
Mine is an old and nameless madness
which nothing ever cures but time.

He is twelve. He sleeps
with his door open,
pleading fear of darkness
except those nights
he takes pillow and blanket
to his closet,
saying he feels his room
too large, hot, bright.
Sleeps as he lives,
hot or cold,
intense, passionate,
ecstatic or in misery,
never content,
his most frequent words
always, and *never*, and *I want*.
Walks outside himself,
slightly to the right,
worlds rushing past,
no one in control,
the son repeating
the mother's childhood
from the inside out

so that I cannot see him
without remembering.

I will not go up the stairs.
Tonight he touched my arm,
wanting the burrito I am saving
for my lunch tomorrow
but will leave for him on the counter
in the morning, though he will not
touch it then. I flinch
from his embraces often.
Not the child I was,
solitary in my hungers,
seeking freedom in aloneness,
he must have crowds,
but I cannot see him without knowing
it is not what comes from outside
which shapes him. The blood
flows in his veins too fast,
nothing in his world stands still,
he wants, wants, wants and nothing
satisfies, nothing can prove to him
that he is loved enough.

It does not help
that I can read his moods
as easily as tell
which way the wind is blowing.
Anyone could read them,
and knowing is not foretelling;
nor can what our folklore
or scientific studies
justify in him give comfort.
I cannot pretend he will
by some swift miracle
outgrow himself as I did not.
Do not mishear me—
I would not call back
his infancy,
not even for the pleasure

of his small hands in fists
beneath my breasts.
For all my milk
I was no natural mother
in that fierce love.
There are no such natural mothers,
only caught ones,
and it is escape I long for.
Not to go back.
Not to undo the past.
In any world, he would repeat me.

Through the elms
the moon casts fragile shadows
on the lawn. I will not
go up and cannot sleep again.
Tonight I dreamed of murder,
then of vultures
with the faces of my husband,
daughter, son,
smiling as they picked my flesh,
though I had done the murdering.
I lay naked as they fed,
could not resist them.
It is an old madness
which my mother knew
and hers before her.
But unlike them
I have warned my daughter,
and I can outwait it.
There is time.
I bore him young.

Conversation

Maria Mullinaux

My daughter asks,
what's the best thing
that ever happened to you?
It is her night to cook,
and I sit on the kitchen stool
which was her favorite place
when she was three, five, nine.

I cannot say,
you, my, daughter.
At fourteen
she knows me better,
already reads *MS.*,
and in a calm voice
won use
of the public school's gymnasium
where winter mornings
she and Lisa
faithfully lift weights.

Living, I say.
She raises her eyebrows,
studies the sauce she stirs,
and I think of the faint trace of whiteness
in the hairline
where a surgeon
eight years ago reclosed my skin,
the right place to have gone in
though he chose it for a vain reason
and would not understand
how important for other labors
the uncut strength of a woman's belly.

Getting older, I try again.
I feel stronger every year.
But I am thinking

how the place
where once there was a uterus
has been freed to function
as a womb
from which daily
I am borne unchained,
what milk I give
called forth by my own will.

She nods.
This summer
she spends her days
between close rows of corn,
stripping the feathery stalks
so the seeds run true,
the only woman there,
her leanness set firmly
against the whistles,
the catcalls
sent to trap her
by the other members
of the crew.
It is hard work,
she tells me.
She is proud
the boys' assaults
wash off so easily,
but she would rather
dream again
of something besides corn.

She laughs,
naming three
who talk
instead of whistling,
then reminds me
as she did at twelve
and nine and five
that she will never marry
but might like a daughter.

There is no malice in her,
only a way of moving
surely
from fact to fact.
Between us
we regret nothing
and I breathe more easily
knowing she can outreach me.

Set the table,
she says,
and don't forget the wine.
From the oven
comes the scent
of fresh bread.

Years Ago I Would Not Have Thought These Fields
Nina Murray

years ago I would not have thought these fields
beautiful
in their muscled grace
unruffled pelts of sheared corn and barley
their ochre languor in the winter sun

I couldn't have imagined
that sadness can be traveled like their paths
until its every ridge and every pebble
becomes my own

the traveler's the only one who's marked
the terrain that's traveled
grates on the eye until the eye becomes
a polished lens
a crystal prism of beauty

so do I venture
into your sorrows
that remain unchanged
unyielding
still

Let Us Speak of a Stone

Nina Murray

let us speak of a stone
on a hushed winter beach far north
where we had once walked
the event
growing irrelevant every day
the rock
fingered by wave
after wave
holds sand in its pores
each grain nestled precisely
as in a dream of a honeycomb

how it must hum
with its illusion of swimming
when the thrusting water rolls
slides above it
retreats
pulls sand from around its waist
bares the roots beneath
the sensation of lift
unmistakably real

each rock alone
senses motion
its knowledge of freedom unseen
unknown
the the other stones
from that distant beach—
the ones we picked
and carried home

Lull

Nina Murray

clouds come like heavy village broads
skirts hiked up expansive thighs clad
in tattered greying cotton
this is infancy again the sodden lap
of someone stepping away from boiling laundry
always the warmest room
the kitchen with tin barrels blueing
wooden tongs steam
of course
tea

I must be waiting to become again
the child who could not be kept in
climbed through windows not to be heard
picked locks never showed up on time from school
and finally left

yes I must be growing up again
squeezed between humid knees
the breath of reeds from the river
combing my hair
the playground swing still in the dark

The Summer the Barn Fell

Charlene Neely

started quietly enough
but in June the rains came

washing all our topsoil off.
July brought a harsh sun.

The recently bared clay
turned to stone so hard a man

and two mules working all day
couldn't force a furrow

and the chickens had more brains
than to peck at its surface

in hopes of a stray bit of grain
or non-existent worms.

It was no great surprise
in August, when the winds came

whistling and howling crosswise
over the burnt fields, chattering

its way through the corn stalks,
demanding everyone and everything

in its way listen to its lengthy talks.
And when that wind changed

to the North removing its support
from the south side of the old barn,

that barn just buckled at the knees
in a sort of prayer to some

higher power, unknown to us.
For days it seemed to beseech

whatever God a barn would embrace.
For what? Salvation? Mercy?

One night with no one around,
no one but the moon,

it just laid down.

Transmogrified

Molly O'Dell

It happens when I float in a tube down
the middle of a river lined with oaks,
sycamores and banks of bluets early
in the season, or jewelweed and black-
eyed Susan later on. I float along
and what I used to call dragonflies dart
every which way: Eastern blue darners,
violet dancers, biddies, and common skimmers.

One lands on my leg. It doesn't
matter what state or which river I float.
What I now know to call a damselfly
lights down on my thigh, holding
her wings above the body, her flight
tentative. I know she'll appear,
I've looked up and learned about
these insects to find some meaning
in this tradition, or maybe it's a ritual;
me and damselfly floating the river
together. I know this is her last instar,
the stage in which she'll reproduce.

She probably hatched this same time
last year and crawled through fall and winter
from weed to stone, clinging to rootlets
when lotic waters grew too strong in spring.
When it was warm enough for me to shed
my gloves and start to fish, she climbed
up on some rock for her last appearance.

On my last float, an American Rubyspot hit
my leg just past the low water bridge
on the cow pasture and stayed on my thigh
for four miles till I landed at the dock.
Then she flew off and hovered while I loaded

my tube in the back seat. When she landed
on the hood, her hind wing caught between
the chrome strip and the paint. She flapped
and flipped to free herself, spiracles fluttering
open and closed till we both rested. My mother
always told me I'd tilt the balance if I touched
a small flying thing. Like a diva composing herself
for a performance, she posed on the hood and slipped
that hind wing from under the strip and vanished.
Seconds later two rubies shimmered above the river
tethered to a ray of afternoon light.

Pollinator

Molly O'Dell

You hover over native waterleaf,
slender stamens and violet petals
sway in your direction.

I watch you work one plant after the other,
your long tongue extracting nectar
honeybees can't reach.

You move to the next wildflower
waving above the forest floor
woven of maidenhair ferns. Bumble

buzz softens as you tune vibrations
to shake pollen from the flower.
Reminds me of my lover trembling

above me. The flowers appear
unscathed. As I head up Hilltop
Trail the nettles sting my legs.

The End of Cheese

Wendy Oleson

Together, there was money
for hunks of Havarti,
chunks of Manchego.
Now, I pay my Mimolette in rent
or to the gas company
or the electric folks.

I could let them turn out the lights,
make my Maytag Blues
find my mouth in the dark,
or meet the mammal smell
of Camembert unencumbered
by the sight of dirty dishes.

But I'm resigned to evenings
without Humbolt Fog.
You are too: alone you eat
cornflakes and see yourself
as something of an ascetic
(except for beer and football).

So we will both grow thin—
which would honestly do us
some good—but if before you waste
away, you find a woman to feed
you cheese, one who bakes
your brie and tops it with cranberry chutney,

I hope she follows with an over-ripe olive.

It's Just a Phase

AJ Pearson-VanderBroek

It's enlightenment! said Buddha—it's self-reliance! cried Emerson—it's hopeless! lamented Nietzsche—it's just a phase, sighed Jesus, and sent me on my way—to find my soul on a brick road buried beneath pavement—I gain a clue, every once in awhile, when red clay bubbles to the surface where tired concrete has worn thin and I think maybe I'm still on the right path—if I jay-walk, will God be pissed? Someone else would be—I'd get a ticket, or the finger (at least) because they don't know where I'm going, just that I'm in the way—where I stand—a poet reciting philosophy beneath the yellow light—the hue of my soul is tainted by their tinted windows—by every Dante that drives past who pens me into various circles of Hell—and I can only imagine how much worse it would be if I skipped class or had sex in a cemetery or was on welfare—if only they knew—(Hello, Brutus)—But is it such a sin if my opinions change with the songs on the radio or if I pay my tithe in tips to the dishwasher in the sloven café on the corner of Central and Sixth or if I think my communion superior, sipping tea in my dingy corner booth reading scripture etched into the table top—it's the artist's way—man versus man, man versus God, man versus nature—but I'm no tragic hero—I'm lost on the sacred street disguised with asphalt and filled with oncoming traffic—just like everyone else—man versus the universe—begging to get hit—and if I don't I'll wake up, I'll stand up, I'll give up and I'll realize it's just a phase.

Alcatraz's Wishing Well

AJ Pearson-VanderBroek

Bereft of pennies, inmate 171 tosses buttons to the bay—because a handful of change would just be turned down—anyway—in the real world—there's never enough money—never enough time—too much to be done—in the cell of individual circumstance—suffocated in metaphorical claustrophobia—that surrounds the open fields taken for granted—burdened by distances—warmed by a sun that is too bright—I'd rather have nothing—than something—that is not quite good enough—just enough health to abuse it—just enough blind faith to look the other way—just enough hope to hand it back—enough pity to notice—the little boy who sits on a broken porch step—collecting rocks in a jar—but not to examine him long enough—to find substance behind his eyes—or see the buttons sprinkled in his gravel—remaining strangers—passersby—never allowing to dispense that which we hold onto—at least, not to those who don't have them too—tokens, souvenirs, memories—recounting times of cars and spotlights—tales of concerts and headlines—on a repeating reel—of song lyrics—that cushion time—and pull shapes out of the fog—instead of looking to the horizon—grasping open sea—we remain heavy—grounded—until we expect to be shrouded in blues and grays—whatever it takes—to fill transparency—console perception—dissolve reality—just so we will never know despair—like the little boy with the empty jar—the day inmate 171—stopped tossing buttons to the bay.

Learning to Swim

Amy Plettner

I witnessed my own death in the trailer park
every Thanksgiving and Christmas
in your parents' living room
as curtains closed in on the morning.
Their large screen blared
on your father's deaf ears
as he bickered with your mother.
Our lives mirrored the edges
of TV trays and beer cans,
as I saw you go down,
so far under,
and I was in the water with you,
yoked to you, the Bible says, by iron.
No longer afraid, dissolving the vow,
I let the silken blanket slip over my skin,
take my chances in the open water.

Letter to Paul in Prison

Amy Plettner

April is a deafening pitch of frogs,
the air loose, the creek skipping high and golden.
In a fit of darkness, coyotes take to the mown path,
and off the dirt road empty beer cans
give way to green along the ditches.
They say a common snipe nested here last May,
her soft eyes all they remember.
The prairies scheduled for fire
to paint it clean and black.
Even the heads of big bluestem,
wind stripped by winter, await combustion.

I stay in a sixty-year-old ranch house,
three miles south of the Denton Daily Double.
My neighbors wave, drive pickups with front loaders,
invite me in come foaling time.
I ask them about the snakes, yellow-bellied racers,
who take over my basement, March and April,
when the nights still forage on frost
and afternoon sun plays to their awakening bodies.
I like to think about them mating below me:
casual, slow, slow twists, and their distinct smell
rising through the register vents. I dream a rainforest.

You can hear prairie chickens across the highway
a vibration not like breath, or hum, or wind in a keyhole,
but more like the sound of that boy we knew
who would rock himself for hours
under the slide at the city park.
The man who knows birds says you can tell
a western meadowlark from an eastern strictly by ear.

The pair of Canada geese horn in low over the pond,
and ducks vanish under the silk surface.
Do you remember that Wednesday?
We climbed Platte Center's water tower—
the village lights, stars scattered at our feet.
Two cans of beer in your sweatshirt pocket
and a runaway moon.

Watching Her Leave in the Dark of Morning

Amy Plettner

Water boils in a glass pan on the electric burner,
orange hot. My daughter's making coffee,
wearing my Australian boomerang sweatshirt
sent from my pen pal in '73,
before I knew there were eggs in my body
making way to this moment.

She says, *Perfect,* off the edge of her cup at 6:30 am,
on her way to my parents, in jeans and a red knit stocking cap,
her insulin pump clipped to her front pocket.
Mom everything is fine she says, as I hear her pants unzip,
toilet flush, the dog's nails clip over the wood floor.

Water freezes in cars overnight, same as people,
three below zero, a tipped over moon.
I've already told her I love her. Three miles away
a passenger train circles a slow track.
My breath startles winter glass.
She honks as she pulls away in her Plymouth Neon.
I wave from the window to her headlights,
close my eyes to make out her face.

Moonlight Ride

Amy Plettner

At sixteen the woman's lost her grip.
She bit her horse on the neck,
roan hairs in the gaps between her teeth.
Grit paves her tongue. She spits.
Spits again. Nothing leaves her mouth.

It was spring,
pelicans on the rough water,
tulips and fists of peony buds,
maples exploding—
his zipper undone,
her skull wedged
under the door handle.

She loves her horse
his bare back
his scent rubbed into her jeans.

She's sorry now.
Grabs a handful of mane,
flings her leg over
to catch the heel of her foot on his hipbone,
boosts into position,
his withers a strange comfort.

My First Morning with Tom Waits

Amy Plettner

October, and Tom is up with the sun,
heat of his breath yellow along my thigh.
I'm a married woman, an adulteress.
Tom doesn't care—
doesn't waste one moment of life
on shame or greed or guilt

    —and I open my legs
around the splendor of his newly wakened face.
Come, I'm a wife,
tired and bored and practiced.

I'd have loved my husband anytime
if he hadn't turned his back,
if he'd let me access,
if he'd entered me the way you do.

Rugged Western Individualism

Diane Raptosh

A man who is his own wife gives birth to his identical twin through his belly button. For months, he thinks it's a cyst. A fistula. An ingrown hair. A fir tree germinating in his spleen. He fathers and mothers this shriven boy, fine and tiny as a walnut lung. With equal parts sweetmeats and a firm touch, he bathes this baby in a small green bowl—that wee, webbed blood of living kin. Nights, the man daubs his chafed nipples with tea bags and lays a wet cloth on his eyes. He tugs at the far left swirl of his mustache.

He sometimes wonders out loud: Is he famished? Is this fullness? When he kisses his own hand, his wife strokes his cheek.

Coda

Caitlin Ray

I wait on the porch for you to drive up
in the silence,
warm wind in my hair.
It is the moment before everything begins.
Tales will be told over the blistering fire for
centuries of this night.
Translations handed down complete
with wars, monsters and gods
but for now, all is quiet.
They are waiting for the signal, in that pause before
the thousands of Greeks
descend on the gates of Troy.
Epic in the way that Rhett swoops in, swirling Scarlett
off her feet,
I'll never go hungry again.
Stories begin in this moment
I look up as each car drives past, and wait.

Abandoned Blossoms

Claudia Reinhardt

The gravel road dead-ends at a yard—
empty, except for cement steps leading nowhere,
like a tombstone marking the plot where a farmhouse
stood for generations, until last June
when clouds swirled green across the pasture;
a tornado clawed open the roof and ripped up the house by its roots.
Weeks later, a bulldozer buried the remains—
shredded curtains, shattered china, a twisted trophy—
the debris of dreams, abandoned by a family that couldn't weather the sadness.
Left behind, the bulbs slept underground in their shelters
where the farm wife had gently laid them. Deep down,
she knew the flowers were extravagant, existing only to be briefly beautiful;
but she planted them anyway
to brighten the path from back porch to barn door.
The house now gone; people moved on,
but the forgotten flowers survived.
And this spring, the daffodils pushed through dark soil near the stairs.
Their ruffled trumpets, yellow as a lark's breast,
exploded into the chill air.

The Untidy Season

Blind Man on the Noon Outbound Bus

Yelizaveta P. Renfro

At first I thought he had a nervous habit
picking away with his fingers
at something in his lap,
but the motion was too meticulous
to be a tick,
an involuntary seizing of the body.
And then I saw in his hand a tool
resembling a small wooden-handled awl
and in his lap a device like a metal sliderule
into which an old piece of junkmail on heavy stock
had been inserted
and through the six-cornered holes in the rule
he rapidly ticked out his words,
writing—what?
A shopping list, a novel, a letter to a friend?

Does he see the words in his mind,
a string of pinholes?
And do we really write the same language
he and I
if he cannot see the butterfly voluptuousness
of a capital B,
the quirky pigtail of the Q,
the slim economy of little l?

I got off the bus before he did
and was sorry to leave him,
his piercing out of words like stitches.
At home I fingered the mail
looking past the letters, the colors
in a card from the local gym,
advertisements for mattresses,
coupons for cleaners,
a notice from the animal hospital,
feeling the smooth surface
for a pattern I could not see.

When I Was Five

Dee Ritter

I learned the names of flowers:
tulip, daffodil, hollyhock, rose
and always the first to arrive—
a purple crocus like a small bruise
on winter's aging face.

The neighbor's wife walked
a mile of slick silt and clay
to show my mother
the small purple bruises
on her submissive flesh.

I learned that bruises
bloom like flowers,
like the first crocus of spring—
like mute testimonials to survival.

The Space Between

Lisa Roberts

for R.G.A.

Between lightning and ground, a rod
spares the house. Between lightning

and thunder, wonder sparks. The moon
from its planet pulls tides of travel across

empty-seeming black. And earth's force
between south and north spins needles,

birds. Lines can go on forever if their tracks
run parallel. Even electrons remain akin

and estranged for atoms' sake. Breach
that space? One line gets lost. Earth flattens

to dust. One bolt blasts one branch,
then consumes whole forests. So you

and I, somewhere between the universal
and atomic, float—without threat

or promise of touch. And stay together
by holding apart. We keep holding

still. At the precise distance for conception.
Neither one flung. Neither one pressed.

Portrait Studies, Days 1 to 22

Lisa Roberts

after Eugene Speicher's *Betalo*

1
The green behind your head
bleeds green veins
into your left hand.
You were real. Are.
How curved the part in your hair.

2
In the portrait gallery, all eyes
stare out. The fencer. The Spanish boy.
A boy in a sailor blouse.
Dead long ago. Alive to me now.

3
Each time I come back, you
show me something new,
today the pomegranate skin
fallen onto your lap.
It must have happened
last night while I slept.

4
Speicher catches her in motion
so different from the others,
who stick flat like coins.
She pivots, about to pull close.
She casts a last look
before twisting, to go.
Only the laughing boy beside her, left,
may dart away, any second,
in any direction—he's loose. Like joy.
But she can only move two directions.
Toward and away. Like love.

5
Monday. Does she notice that I haven't come?

6
When I arrive today, the abstract background
is on the move. Green shadow infects
your white blouse. The upright
scythe swings. Pink oil slick
oozes close, from the left.
You shrink.
       The blood floor rises.

7
I've decided that he loved her.
Loved the face he pulls my gaze
away from to send it down
a white shoulder, a white sleeve
to land on a green vein. The hand
with the black onyx ring. Her lap
where pomegranates collect. Loved
the upper right swoop she made him make.

8
A gallery spotlight, above left,
so when I crouch right, look up,
she dissolves—all painter's motion.
One long curve along
an inside sleeve. Multiple short strokes
cup a breast. On the head
a crown of high paint ridges.
Shine bumps along the tight
mechanical grid. I'm close,
low. Glance up at the living eye
of the camera. Then rise. Step
back four paces. Again
she floats to the surface.

9
The canvas is a face. Pores. Planes.
Skin stretched tight across a bone frame.
Senseless. Until the artist draws its breath.

10
Artists' oil suspends the dead.

11
Last Wednesday, the black cushion
was starting to break apart, light
from dark. But when I
came today, you showed me
pink and beige flesh
from her face, splattered
onto the tuft. Your most
important gift so far.

12
Sunday. Her thinned face. Hungry ghost.

13
Awful to look in that face.
    I'll follow the bounce of pliant
crescents along the scalp,
    watch parabolas echo shoulders—
reverse. Better. Now I catch
    the long smudge between wall and floor
at double dutch with the stitched cord
    between blouse and skirt. Like this
I let lines play. Like this
    I break the gaze of her grasp.

14
Saturday. Above a shoulder, right:
three hairs from his brush.

15
From deep abstraction, he draws her out.
From all the sea forgets, all the blood doubts,
he spares opaque light that swirls
a green idea of a wall, a red idea for a floor.
I watch. What he does next I don't know
how to follow. Green thoughts collect
shadows along the mouth, shadows

beside the brow to project
her nose, her forehead. Solid.
Speicher swipes chromium oxide
and fills all her live volume,
as my heart breaks.

16
Painter, teach me how to make.

17
Madder root. Cochineal beetle.
Zinc. Peat. Hog bristle.
    Rabbit skin. Malachite.
    Cow's urine. Ripe
flax. Fumes from vinegar,
fumes from horse manure:
    lead flakes. Burnt bone,
    burnt horn. Burnt grape.
Dirt. From Verona,
from Siena. Dirt
    from Box Elder, Montana.
    Minnesota's Blue Earth River.
Cork and soot and pitch and bark.
Rise up. Do your work.

18
Bones burn in her pupils' pit,
her lashes, brows catch the soot.
Crushed insects hatch the pink
in her lips. Madder roots in her cheek.

19
I want to reach beyond the image,
dig into paint, shred
canvas with my claws, clasp
your living hand with green blood
in my hand still alive and plunge
both into my chest. Speicher
makes me think I can.

20
The artist tastes her face with his brush.

21
She is breaking up. Part in her hair
aimed toward the upper green swoop.
Face crumbling onto the tuft.
Background is taking over. Chunks
of bloody floor cancel her black lap.

Or does she resist both
dissolution and invasion,
to remain, for now,
beautifully composed
and beautiful?

22
The face is so tender.
Maybe he didn't love her.

NOTES
Betalo is held by The Sheldon Museum of Art in Lincoln, Nebraska.

Many texts contributed to my knowledge of painters' materials: *Artists'
Pigments: A Handbook of Their History and Characteristics*, volumes
1–3, edited by Robert Feller, Ashok Roy, and Elisabeth West Fitzhugh;
Lac and the Indian Lac Research Institute by Dorothy Norris, P.M.
Glover, and R.W. Aldis; *The Artist's Handbook* by Ray Smith; and
Colors from the Earth by Anne Wall Thomas.

Young Lady

Lisa Roberts

Have a good day, young lady, he says
handing over my change and a wry smile
that shows how well he knows I'm long past young,
was probably never a lady, and that
my chances for having a good day
just got worse.

      And he's not alone.
Other men have offered some small kindness,
opening a door, setting bread on a table,
served up with this now familiar compliment-curse,
young lady, as if I'll love any lie that flirts
with restoring what I must prize most.

      What they
don't know and this man can't guess?
I do not want to be young again. To dutifully
perform the job of making men, like him,
want me. Just when age is lifting me out of sex
like that and putting me someplace else
I haven't named yet. It's a high and windy place
where I climb sometimes. And I remember
that there other people's names for me
can't follow. An invisible middle
of everywhere. A latitude inexhaustible.

Within

Marge Saiser

When I was lodged within my mother
I floated as she walked to work,
bobbing at anchor, insulated from any bump in the road,
and later wedged in tightly, not able to stretch,
well-fed, warm in an upside-down world.
You, too,
floated in your water world,
finishing at last with that space, or lack of it,
squeezed through an aperture,
not to be upside down much again
except a time or two in the grass,
rolling head over heels—small remnant.
By our own biped laws walking
as soon as we are able, the liquid world
shut to us except as swimmers, visitors
to pools or to oceans, and perhaps
with luck and planning to a small flotation chamber,
forty dollars per hour, darkness, nakedness,
water in which large quantities of salts
have been dissolved, a door to close
for an hour, body floating face-up,
water the temperature of the skin,
ears below water listening only to water,
hearing the breath in,
the breath out,
and also the small drum of the heart.
No wonder we want this dark chamber—
and fear it—water holding the body,
our own pulse an approximation of the drum
of the mother's heart, first music,
the beat she always had for us, walking to work,
walking home again, hungry or tired in the world
we eventually come into, when the time comes.
The attendant knocks on the door. The hour's up.

And the body rises,
opens with its own two hands the door,
and there is light now. The body emerges and begins:
shower, dress, and—because it's time—
return to the world of work.

Artifact

Marge Saiser

At the museum,
I walk among displays:
beaded moccasins and arrowheads.

I think about women
dropping meat
into boiling water,

feeding children
corn or hope or milk,
a mother opening her garment

so a baby can suck his fill,
his head between the warmth of her body
and the skin of the deerskin dress.

In a hospital room,
standing at the sink
on my substantial legs,

I wash my mother's dentures,
scrubbing
uppers and lowers,

artificial pink
artificial white
under running water.

My dripping fingers
place her teeth
into a curved plastic dish,

and I carry it,
an offering,
toward her bed.

Poem of Thanks
after Thomas Lux
Marge Saiser

Thank you, Whoever,
for these women I'm singing with.
Thank you for syllables
intoned. For the song, thank you, and for the feet
we stand on to sing it,
feet that move us around a circle we have
imagined. We break its imagined perimeter:
some step in, some step out. Thank you,
Whoever, for the stepping
and for the *in*
and the *out*. For the song, and
for whatever language
our teacher teaches us to sing it in.
Are you listening, Whoever, how I
make up some words, how I sometimes
hum or lip-sync? Here beside the frozen river
a handful of women in a circle sing *shalom*
over and over. Here beside the ice
and beside the hidden current. Here beneath trees
without leaves and without birds.
Here beside the fire we have lit,
before we take whatever food we brought
out of whatever we brought it in. Here before we feast,
we lift our hands in the center
of a circle we fabricate,
breath going in, breath going out.
Thank you, Whoever, for
this song we sing to one another.

Changing Sheets

Nancy Savery

This holy ritual of
our grandmothers,
stripping soiled sheets,
shaking out
weeks of cares, hurts, interrupted
slumber,
airing pillows on the porch
in early morning chilled air,
fluffing them,
pressing noses into their coolness,
inhaling the breezy scent,

stretching clean linens
tautly over corners,
pulling on crisply ironed cases,
re-assembling loving order to the bed
with fresh layers of
cleanliness,
saintliness,
and dreams.

Our Sin

Jeanne Schieffer

I knew he was there, huddled
like a Boy Scout in the dark.
The flashlight made his face a mask
Touch me...there. And I did,
thinking he'd smile at me across
the dinner table. *Now...this.*
And I tried, but I didn't do it
right, he said. On the couch,
under blankets, in the car's backseat,
I obeyed as a good little sister should.
Harlequin paperbacks told lies
of sweet, wet kisses and fiery hands
on breasts. But the kiss I asked for
was dry as sand. I burned our sin
in Sunday school, watched
the paper fold into charcoal flecks,
breathed deep the smoke
and forgave us both.

It Looks Worse Than It Is

Barbara Schmitz

I should have said to
my guests to distill their concern
over my hobble, my crookedness
when I tried to stand straight.

It's just my bent ancestors
swooped down for one more
whiff, one more glance
at the daily life of coffee,
kolache, eggs with lots of cheese.

I'll chase them on their
heavenly ways after a bit,
after they've had a totter
around the place, sniffing
snow fall and late January
blooming pink on house plants.

I'll straighten, walk on into
my own life by afternoon, letting
them continue up eternity's
ladder, advancing, while I dither
away the remains of my time
glancing out windows, scribbling notes,
wondering what's for dinner.

Keeping Silence

Barbara Schmitz

When we could speak again—
after a week—we found we really
had nothing much to say. All those
nuggets dropping off our tongues
did not grow into golden coins;
the witty pearls cascading did
not spring up as vivid flowers.

Our mutterings and murmurs
were mostly shavings, splinters
of distracted thought, useless
and better left unnoticed, ungathered,
as we passed by.

Night Watch

Morgan Songi

Eerie music of coyote chorus,
and the cries of mountain lions
like children lost in the night.
The cattle, uneasy, mill
restlessly in the corral.

My father grabs the flashlight,
and heads down the basement stairs,
I run to catch up. It's too hard
to stay in the house—and wait—
after the screen door slams
and the flashlight beam disappears,
when the sound of the wind
and the ticking of the clock
make me feel sick.

It's easier to go out into the night
where the wind whips across my face
and every sound is the footfall of a cat
with lashing tail and teeth bared
in an impersonal snarl.

Easier, when even after I'm back
in the house with the basement door
closed behind me, the tiny hairs on my neck
stay prickly because it feels like
something is watching.

Although the night is warm, I shiver,
pull the comforter up around my ears
and try to sleep, while cattle press
against the fences of my dreams, and out
in the north pasture ravine
a mountain lion screams.

Cold War

Morgan Songi

I
Do not imagine
birches, bent and trailing silver,
echoing crystal laughter.

Do not think.

II
Fear
flows through the landscape
like a scorched riverbed.
My passion buried alive,
rots and longs for death
while I see only too well,
but none too soon,
that having come to love,
I stayed to wound.

III
Divorce.
Word like a corpse,
you bloat and grow,
take on grotesque reality,
and crowd the empty space
of what started out as *marriage.*

Like a fragment
of fractured bone,
or a mouthful of ground glass,
you come, full-blown
into the room,
without my ever
saying a word.

IV
My silence,

a hibernation of the heart,
riding out winter,
while shattered dreams
kaleidoscope northern light.

My Goddaughter Asks Me to French Braid Her Hair
Judith Sornberger

Mothers fail so much when you're fourteen.
Take Zoe's mom, who can't French braid her hair.
Take me, who couldn't keep my sons from smoking
or dropping out of school. But that was once
upon a grim time when I'd turned into the witch.
I mean, Zoe complains, *she can, but it comes out
all loose and lopsided—pathetic.*
Louise shrugs, says she suggested Zoe ask me,
and I feel like the girl whose father
claims she can spin gold from straw.
Sure, I'll try. But my fingers, entering that satin,
tremble as they weigh the chance of failure,
for I've never attempted such a thing.
But motherhood—even one as tenuous as this—
brims with such moments of bravado.

Long ago Louise and I weighed
pros and cons of her becoming pregnant.
Barely surviving my boys' adolescence,
I was full of dark portents. Thank God she ignored me.
Zoe's light brown strands are sleek as corn silk,
and I hold on, as to the reins of an impish filly,
but not, I hope, too tight. I separate the hair
into three ropes and soon fall under the spell
of this plaiting—the over and under
and over of our whispers and giggles.
With this small feat, I'm making three wishes:
Just this once to outshine the mother,
whose largesse lifted such silk into my hands;
to watch the daughter beaming
for one moment in her mirror;
and to weave myself into their story.

Way Station
Judith Sornberger

Love, why must you grieve
that our parents never visited this home,
this joy we've found?
True, death swooped down
for each father and each mother,
one by one, in rapid succession
like the chickadee, then the grosbeak
then the bully-boy blue jay,
landing on our feeder that perches
between lawn and mountain wildness.

Why, you ask, couldn't they have lived
to watch the birds, raccoons, and deer
from our back deck where worlds meet
and mingle at woods' edge
and red squirrels regularly crash the party.
Look at that one leaping on the tray,
chattering its scorn as it scatters
doves paused there.

Imagine how pissed off your mom would be.
Shit-asses! she'd shriek, tearing off her sandal,
aiming at one like she used to do in her backyard.
Can't you hear your father's throaty chuckle,
like the gurgle of the small stream
in our backyard after rainfall?

And, when she misses, his voice raucous
as the red-winged blackbird's,
daring her to try the other one.
Then her shrill command that he climb up
and fetch it, which he does.
Still, when he returns, offering the shoe
with a mock flourish, she swats him with it.
Always such silly squabbles were their love calls.
And can't you see my mother lounging

The Untidy Season

161

on a chaise, waving her cigarette as she talks,
her smoke pluming toward heaven—
high priestess of the patio?
She, who even in Omaha suburbs
warned her daughters to beware of bears,
hopes, we know, that one will drop by.

Which reminds Dad of the time
my little sister said she was so strong
she could beat up a bear. *Hello, zoo?*
my father says, holding his hand phone
to his ear, as he did that day.
Say, this is Bill Mickel over on 86th Street.
Could you please send over
your biggest, meanest bear?
Can the creatures nearby tell
our laughter from our crying?

I suppose it must sound funny
when I greet the bright blood slash
of the cardinal each morning.
Hi, Mom! I call to the bird
that always cheered her.
Do I believe she hears me?

When we call out to the dead, my love,
don't our own words proclaim they're here?

Why I Have Not Told You I Love You

Sara Lihz Staroska

1. Beer slicked and hungry
my tongue cannot be trusted
inside my own mouth.

2. Holding my tongue
propels me forward. In the dungeon
I work in, when my heat is shut off,
when I wake up
to my cat playing
little spoon to my aching body,

I will tell you tomorrow.

3. When we went camping,
I got lost. My shoes sopping, swatting
at mosquitoes, you found me
and stole my flashlight.

"Look," you said.
"It's Venus," and the goddess
lit my tongue.

"I," I began,

and you thought
I was talking about myself again,

so you listened.

4. What if I'm wrong? I am
more plastic bag than bird.

You are a rock. And some days
a slingshot, but I have been blown from here
before, been snared by tree branches
and windshield wipers. I am full
of holes, love. What if I cannot hold you?

Weeks of Silence

Sara Lihz Staroska

My sister has not spoken in three weeks;
the daily swallowing
of her own tongue
looks so much like choking
I can barely breathe to watch her,

but on Tuesday, when it was just us
she cleared the rock that rolls across the cave
of her mouth. Her eyes bloomed at the world.
Tree stumped, she stared
    You   are   the only
but not at me.

There is a field of small things
before her. My teeth are an audience of moonflowers,
my earrings are fireflies.
    You   are   the only   only   bird
She mouths the words
to a song we both know.
    You   are   the only   bird
    in this blue sky   flying backwards
Dad says
she's just grinding her teeth.

Harvest

Mary Stillwell

Each summer before we moved to the farm,
my stepfather, aided by Miracle-Gro,
turned weeds and clay into a productive garden
in the vacant lot behind our house, where
one autumn, my neighbor Mike and I wove
brittle sweet corn stocks into a latticework of walls
and a dome laced with discarded peanut plants
and hybrid pumpkin leaves. At night, we slipped
between the stalks to smoke his mother's Salems.
They made us giggle and dizzy. Then we stretched
side by side on our bed of leaves, ash and cottonwood,
to watch the sky and its stars edging through the sheaves
overhead, and contemplated the days ahead as best
we could with our limited supply of information,
listening to the vesper sparrows settling down,
imagining how, in the morning, we might fly away,
not touching each other for fear we would ignite.

Black Cardinal

Mary Stillwell

Morning's milk warms the horizon,
and in that first hint of light,
the male cardinal, black against a field
of husks, pecks for seeds at the base
of the bare ash tree. The female, lovely
in her paisley shawl, is sleeping.

When the milk spills blue onto the roofs,
his beak, crest, his heart-shaped body
rust, and I'm reminded that the sun,
a mother who lives on the other side
of the world, visits her daughter
nearly every day for lunch. It's not
my story to tell, but by the end,
a rattlesnake turns the daughter
into a redbird. "Kwish! Kwish!
Kwish!" she calls from the bushes.

Each spring the cardinal courts
his love, offering her the seed
from his beak. She thinks
he wants to fox-trot and they do,
for a moment, before she extends
her tufted head and they kiss.

Back then, had all gone as planned,
our ancestors might have returned
from Ghost Country. Instead, dead
remain dead, and the male cardinal
waits under the feeder. As she shakes
open her shawl, he bursts into flame.

Summer Whites

Carla Stout

Here is your list, my friend,
of frenetic ways to say good-bye to
summer. I walk from a shower of
regrets, barefoot into fall
and into summer's failing twilight,
pressing the back of my white eyelet
nightgown to bricks that hold onto heat a
little longer, storing up their fire for the
next thunder snow. And I huff white
jasmine, white moonflowers and white
four o'clocks hoping their perfumes will
ignite me and mock time once again
before I climb into the gray briar that is
winter. And how the whites prevail over
the darkest I planted. I kiss them,
taste them till I am wrecked by their creeping
insinuations and braid them into my wet
hair and garland them around my damp
neck. On paler skeins
of clouds, a white mask glides above trees,
teasing me with the face of a mime, pleasing
me with the face of a man.

There, nighthawk. There, incubus,
saving white mist in Andromeda, are
you the one to ransom me from winter?
Tell me your name
and I will write it, drive it, read into it,
a red abiding sun, midsummer night undone.

Things to Count On

Mary Strong Jackson

on the woman next door
to step into my morning in red bathrobe
    and a
breeze to lift her black hair
so it licks across her face

on color
    the way
her blue-eyed dog
dips his head for just seconds
to conclude again if this peaceful pause
is the morning ritual of our yesterdays
    I count on the
color of his gray and white coat
outlined in black to cut crisp around cool air
    and his sniff
through the yard
as he counts interlopers who traversed the night
counting coup and leaving their scent

I count on slow run-on sentences
and mixed metaphor talkers
who watch to see if I dip in my head in ritual

on moments when the breeze lifts the lilacs scent
and trees wise
as shamans speak poetry
to an endless sky

    I count your
breath
waltz against my neck

unfinished   unrefined   impossible

The Devil Came to My House to Install a Satellite Dish

Tammy Trucks-Bordeaux

I've warned my husband over and over to avoid the conversations,
but he cannot hide his Indian face when he comes to a customer's door.
Some customers are curious about our culture.
Some, however, see the Devil, but even with the Devil in the room, they still will
sacrifice a few hours with one of us for the cooking, or sports channel.
Some are Christians and warn him of the dangers of our shifty, pagan ways,
and he honestly claims he tries to avoid them.
They are always the ones, as he pulls out the cables, his tools, who follow him
around and speak the fear of Pantheism, further lengthening his stay and misery.
"Is that what they call it?" he asked me.
"Yes, they think we're worshipping nature. You know, they think we
    worship trees. It's called Pantheism." "Besides, isn't God supposed to
    do the judging?" I asked him.
"Yeah, they forget about that."

Here we are on another Saturday morning trying to have a quiet
breakfast of cinnamon French toast,
and I'm listening to the latest Battle of the Little Big Horn.
I pour some syrup and ask him why he even bothers with pointless
    confrontations over beliefs.
"You're just scaring them," I tell him. "Talk about dogs or the weather."
"I'm just trying to tell them the truth about our religion," he explains.
"Don't bother," I said. "They think we're the Devil."

Well, except for that one nice woman he once met, I thought.
One day when he walked into her house,
she had pictures all over her walls of Indians on horses.
They had a nice conversation about the culture.
My husband paused and looked around.
She apologized and said, "I hope you're not offended."
My husband said, "No, not at all."
"Back home on the reservation we have pictures of farmers on tractors
    hanging all over our walls."

Meteor Showers

K. Denise Wally

Earthbound mineral being
Hurtling suicidal through the atmosphere
A blaze of splendor
In a beautiful ceiling of stars
You are the twinklers

Unfurling forth with furor
Tersely projecting through electrons, ozone and nitrogen
Propelled by gravity and other attractions
Frozen rock
Ignited bright in my line of sight

Tonight I shall take a meteor shower
And wash my hair with stars
Lather my body with auroral lights
And dry off on the Mons of Mars
I shall moisturize with nebulae
And perfume with the dust of moons
I shall dress in the swirls of galaxies
And wear the sun in my hair at noon

You Drew a Picture of Us

Susan Warren Utley

you drew a picture of us
two young lovers, single heart
now strangers contemplate its worth
critique the lines and call it art

i composed a poem about us
shared my lover, shared my friend
now strangers cannot get enough
they want your art, they want my pen

you painted portraits of us
they hang upon a gallery wall
now strangers scrutinize your work
dissect our lives and see it all

i composed a story about us
shared some secrets, shared some pain
now strangers stop me with their pens
write to a friend and sign my name

you took a photograph of us
bared our bodies, bared your soul
now strangers flock and stare at us
and the innocence you stole

i wrote angry words of us
scrawled where everyone could see
now strangers revel in our pain
and they call it poetry

you burned my writing in the trash
i pulled your artwork from the wall
now strangers point up to the sky
as they watch your paintings fall

we did an interview of us
and they told us what to say
now strangers think they know our pain
they hit pause, rewind, replay

i wrote an apology to us
counted words and placed the ad
now strangers toss it in the bin
recycled news they call us sad

you said you're sorry about us
graffiti mural on a wall
now strangers pause and shake their heads
refuse to call it art at all.

The Flexible Anorexic Considers Her Extremities

Kathleene West

The feet are so cold they
burn—clammy fire licking at my
arches smoldering the bone,
these ephemeral body parts
a phantom
      hovering over my ankles
         in a parody of pain.

I can deal more easily with the frigid hands.
The TV yogini demonstrates
      how to rub, rub them together
      then massage the heat
         into my wrists,
         arms, shoulders.

"Little monkey paws,"
      he said of her hands
meant to be an endearment.
      Remember the story? The ghastly paw
      a source for three wishes
         Be careful what you ask for
         You might get it
                  an old wives' tale in
                 all the tongues of
                 the world.

Like Christ suffering the little children
my hands cup dank air,
      each line on the palm a frozen canal
      criss-crossing the nether lands,

"Your circulation fails you,"
my dearest boy says, illiterate
      in history
         or palmistry.

It is he who fails me
forgets me
    as a fig tree might forget
    its obvious symbolism

and present itself
merely as a tasty comestible
dried or ripe.

The Flexible Anorexic Watches Him Walk Out the Door

Kathleene West

She has nothing to blame
but her own unsavory self,
the near-beer juices
she secreted, the bouillon sweat,
rancid tears.

As she trimmed her body to fit
his lean shadow, she exulted: *At
last I am thin enough*

to lock her thighs
inside his hipbones
to lean the cage of her back
against the shallow dish of his kneecap.

She would demonstrate
how she worked
the kinks that plagued her
with the fish pose, the locust, crow—
fat-feathered, insistent as a black death.

"God help you," they say
in some countries, after a sneeze.
Five centuries is not so long. Dame
Hunger turns in
her visitor's card, starvation melts
like a cherry popsicle
and appetite returns to whet
a comfortable desire.

He slips from her skinny soul

and sniffs out
something substantial,
a good woman
with meat on her bones.

Notes at Close of a Winter Day

Rachel Naomi West

None of my plans came through—it was
the snow.

In the cold of my workshop nothing seemed feasible
and nothing worked, only
the coffee pot
and suchlike pleasures—
also the task of moving the snow—

these things I did.

My true love called on the telephone
and didn't even complain
about his woman, didn't say her name.
Instead he showed me photographs
of himself and I said *Yes,
you are beautiful.*

I missed a number of parties as well.

Instead, because of the snow
and the overwhelming solitude of my heart
that knows no better company,
I stayed at my mother's house,
shoveled the walk,
made the tea, the coffee.

I was trapped and distracted myself
in being helpful.

Picking Strawberries
Roca, Nebraska

Ruth Williams

One in the bucket,
one in my mouth. I ate them
with dirt, ate
until my throat was raked.

My mother told me I inherited a taste.
The acid: a stinging champagne.

The tender skin of my mouth
dotted with red pulp, tiny seeds
burrowed between teeth. A little hardness
to occupy the tongue.

I would eat more as we left for home.
I would eat as we washed them at the sink,
as we hulled their stems.

Those nights, I dreamt
I gulped, swallowing
into a red hangover.

I woke. My mouth open and opening.
I'd inherited a taste for air.

Norway

Ruth Williams

> *I told her…*
> *that there's something wrong with the expression*
> *one always holds the harpoon alone.*
> —Aase Berg, "Core"

The winter lengthens. This blank horizon is a way
of being more profound than snow. Inside it, a lantern
swatch of yellow curling over a buried leg.

In pioneer days, they'd tie frozen
bodies to the fencepost. The twine a way of
waiting for spring.

It is a way of lengthening.
I have fallen into repeating myself.
Legs in a grim frozen season.

I Had to Work

Ruth Williams

myself into it. That was definite.
Motorized hand, your slack soul of slip.
Our wonder bread of white blanche.

I am obsessed with the sponge of our language.
Squeeze-box for my longing, arbiter
of my ruler-run tongue.

Portioned out, the words wick their golden
flax color along the page and
make themselves known only to God,

the reader. God, the reader! If your
clavicle comes in contact with me. If
your earlobe meets me, then I will. I will

do myself unto you, twin, twine, the
shipyard that aggregates the boats, I will be
specific, a definite blue harbor

to your waved plenitude.

Getting Through

Karen Wingett

I. Air
Petunias sicken in their potting soil,
nearly killed by psychotic weather,
floods, straight-line gusts, humidity.
I inhale thickly, remember a steamer
when I was ten, down with pneumonia,
fever high as yesterday's heat index.

I think of my mother in her casket,
her first airless summer, too hot
in the green wool blazer I chose,
the lawn above her choked by crabgrass,
something she always hated,
and would now if she still knew how.

II. Clouds
My mother sits in the living room
with her flashlight and faux crocodile purse
listening to the weather radio
waiting for the tornado, ready
to seek shelter in the damp basement
along with the sterling silver flatware,
and cut (not pressed) glass lemonade set.

The green horizon crackles in the west.
She asks my dad if he wants to take
his war books downstairs. He smells the rain
and laughs, Out of the way of the tornado!
as he descends the stairs with his tote
of memories, aerial photographs
of Normandy, Paris, Nazi factories.

He returns to survey the sky, neighbors
telling of a funnel cloud near Hartington.
He puts the car out of harm's way, walks through

thick perfume of lilies of the valley
just as wind startles the hydrangeas,
blowing purple petals into the air
like tiny Roman candles at dusk.

III. Perhaps
Perhaps I can't turn Alzheimer's into poetry,
its vagueness hovering, unspecific.
But hallucinations are beautiful in their horror,
grotesque metaphors: woman sitting on the edge
of a bed, Poof, she's dust in the trash,
the lady who shows up at midnight, feet bent backwards,
grotesquely twisted, Picasso-like,
the massacre near Pukwana on Red Lake,
Satan in a nurse's face.
And the richness of the babble:
This is the forest primeval,
Where is God? helphelphelphelp,
Do we have to sing? No great intellects
here. P-38s on the lawn, miles to go before I sleep,
and the tangled lyric about the daughter
becoming the mother who's going to sew
new clothes, make snickerdoodles,
but can't find a way to take her home.

IV. Leaves
Her ivy mourns its way through crevices
into the empty mid-century house
like a toddler abandoned in the yard
searching, crazy with loneliness,
reaching into eaves, clinging to sidewalk,
smashing its leaves into the east window,
grabbing at the screen door, looking for life,
feeling the desertion, frantic. The vines
find new mischief, once forbidden places.
They wiggle into the forsaken mailbox,
cover the unread gas meter,
intrude upon fading purple irises,
crawl all over and under themselves,
overwhelmed by a need to be mothered again.

Ancestor

Laura Madeline Wiseman

When I remember the still life, I remember light
from a window and a woman. She'd just been

called away. One nude foot steps from the frame.
A callused curve of heal exposes a patina of dirt.

But in the still life there's no window. No woman.
Only a room with a wood floor, green walls, a chair

in the corner. The kind moved room to room to serve
in other ways. A spot it would never be, not like this.

Nothing else there but the chair and a long shadow.
It's clear it's a woman's chair because it lacks arms.

Across the seat rests a white apron trimmed in lace.
One tie loops around the chair leg, no longer bound

around her hips. The apron holds a pail of sun-
warmed peaches. One peach has fallen out.

A moment ago she removed the apron and fled
the fruit in this lonely room. Why do I want her

not to return, but to continue to wherever she's going
into the world, in the window, that none of us can see?

Fishing

Laura Madeline Wiseman

I.
At mid-afternoon, everything could be seen
from the dock and the wood-lined shore

as if the water, several feet deep,
were a scrim, a fantastical line,

which has been agreed upon
by those around you.

The dock floated on the lake
down the hill from the cabin.

The water, even with the tread of feet,
remained still and clear, above the pebbles,

fish, and strands of plants
anchored to the bottom.

II.
At even intervals eyes ache
from the strain of looking

at computers or a whiteboard
that has grown fuzzy.

The doctor will scold, say,
You need to take more breaks,

and offer a prescription more intense
than the last and more costly.

You want to ask, when he takes his light
and flashes it through the jelly

what can be seen
of the retina, the floaters,

because you've been raised on the belief
that your body is translucent in any light,

that everything inside
is there for the hook.

Connubial Plight

Laura Madeline Wiseman

I am trying to redefine marriage, to get the word to zing,
rumba, and twine. But matrimony and its accoutrements

are verbs fixed in the future or past. *I will be affianced.*
Or, *We married on Tuesday in an Arizona courthouse.*

And, *We consummated our love!* Such conjugal verbs
rarely reside in the present. There's no *engages* or *sexes.*

Even the *wedding* is a concrete noun and *marrying* too.
Indeed, my spousal ceremony lasted all of five minutes.

I in a flowered blue summer dress, sandals, and a hat.
My bridegroom in a plaid button down with cargo shorts.

Wedlock is a word bound in white stays and lace ribbons
where the subject receives the action. *I am betrothed to him.*

I will be lead to the altar. We will be joined and made one.
Even to speak of marriage I use the conditional voice,

My Adam, should we have a child, be fruitful and multiple?
Or, *Darling, do you want to have oral sex or intercourse?*

It's been years since our honeymoon and still we're yoked
in our state of nuptial bliss, though we don't go on dates

because there's no definition for dating after tying the knot.
My *Roget's Thesaurus,* copyrighted in 1922 and 1991,

offers options for the hymeneal union, like *man and wife.*
And though *marry* is the primary verb, it is followed by

wive, to take to oneself a wife, espouse, and *be spliced.*
The wedded pair can both be a *spouse,* but only the husband

can be a *partner, mate, man,* or *consort.* The wife, alas,
is the *better half, helpmate, lady, matron,* or *squaw.*

The language couples us: a mated pair. Two left hands
meet in a place where new words are just beginning to form.

Of Air, Water, and Wings

Julie Wrasse Van Winkle

It was you that had created this stirring,
or created this monster,

as it would later be referred to.

It was your eyes—brown and soft as a doe's—yet
harboring a fierce flame that burned straight through me.

I needed you like I needed air.

I was too weak to loose myself from your grip or
I would have cast myself into the sea
and let the ocean's belly have a crack at me

and Air would become obsolete.

Or perhaps the ocean would swallow only the beast brewing inside
spitting back an angel to wash upon the shore
leaving only the mystery of air
and me,
needing nothing but wings.

Beauty

Julie Wrasse Van Winkle

I used to know beauty like an old friend
She came to my door and I let her in
She stained my lips deep cherry red
And opened my mouth up like a valentine

When I was fifteen she came again
She laid breasts upon my skin
Unfamiliar as two stones in my chest I carried them

Legs
Hips
Breasts
Lips
Spilling over me like milk
My little darlings
Oh cheeky girl
I could eat you up

Beauty returned and gave me hips like a purse
I opened them
Letting my pearls spill out

My long limbs met loveliness next
Two towers of yellow heat
They were the way in and the way out

Rigor on National Coming Out Day, Lincoln, Nebraska, 1996

Sandy Yannone

I've been pacing
the circumference
of my classroom
for weeks,
rambling
about story,
about the fictive
line
between
truth
and dare
and rubbing
my hands
together
with broken
sticks of chalk,
preparing them
to grip
some thought
like a high bar.
Caked white,
my hands
alone
can't unveil
their desires
for certain
motions,
so I smack
my hands
against
the board
leaving
my prints
that include

traces
of other
women's
bodies.
They replace
the words
they could write
like the chalk
outline
of the corpse
replaces the body,
and I remember
my back
pressed
against
the blacktop
after school
and her insisting
Lie still.
Don't move,
as she ran
the new stick
of stolen chalk
around
my edges,
her fingers
blushing
against me
as I became
one long,
curving
line.
After,
she extended
her hands
and pulled me
from the second
dimension.
Can I draw

some clothes?
I asked
peering over
myself.
No, she said,
You'll make
a mistake,
and I don't want
to trace you again.
But the fact is
she did. Today
after class
I avoid the hate
chalked
under each step
I take on
the campus sidewalk.
Next to those words,
the chalk
outlines of bodies
the world
wants to negate.

Thin Objects

Sandy Yannone

The order is not
important
in retrospect.

You can admit
the women
who induced

your dizziness,
your shortness
of breath

are now small
trinkets you no longer
deny you collect.

They dangle
from your wrist, dancing
without partners.

Sometimes one
smacks hard
between your skin

and another
solid object: a countertop,
the car door, the bedpost.

In the morning's pinch
tiny bruises flower, smart
to the touch.

But you never determine
which one struck
the tinny blow:

the woman
who lurks all night
around the details

of the first woman
who asked
to kiss you

who whispered
into the first minutes
of the new day,

"We can't ever talk
about this
again,"

the woman
who wouldn't talk
for months

until the Friday afternoon
you arranged
to eat fish

for a non-coastal lunch,
and not even
the woman before

your body knew
there could be
women,

who went to Italy,
returned with a charm
of the Pope,

which at first glance
you mistook
for an Eisenhower

dime, blessed,
in a brown, velvet box.
She offered the alloy,

then
withdrew
herself.

They are all
ornament now,
shiny and smooth

like coins
comforting your pockets,
resting against places

where you can feel
your bones
refuse.

What the Woman Who Doesn't Measure Will Do

Sandy Yannone

The ruler's little slashes form a ladder
she will not climb: the shadow of a shadow
forming on the steps, the steps themselves,
the light, the ocean that should keep still.

She dives underwater. Her hands retrieve many stones,
small bodies she piles on the bank when she returns for air.
Later, she will throw each cold stone back
against the pane of all the windows she's wanted

to break. They will sink farther from her
than the first time they sank. Unattended,
the moon burrows into the blue. *Far away*, she says
as if no instrument could fathom such distance.

What the Tooth Remembers

Sandy Yannone

The permanent front tooth lay ashamed,
brown and rotten in my stronger hand
in the dream where we had neighbors
who cared if our family was alive
and intact, if the paint on the house's north side
started to chip and what color
we might reconsider. And they cared
if the mail accumulated in its box,
if the milk in its glassy ships
went sour on the docks of our front porch,
so when I thought to escape
the pitch black of my bedroom
to find my always 29-year-old mother,
I knew to head for the neighbors.
They would have her in a wooden chair
on the closed-in back porch, pouring her
cup after cup of coffee, wishing
she would never leave. I winced
the window open and set my hands
against the screen. Garbled voices traveled
across our dark yards and burrowed
into my palms. Through the pine trees,
my eyes could barely find the candied plastic
lights strung against their house.
But the neighbors, all they could do was think
about the future, how to convince my mother
to visit again tomorrow. More coffee? No,
perhaps the homemade wine.
While all this time, the tooth is still
here, living out its life in Lincoln, Nebraska,
sutured into my mouth seventeen long years ago
after I killed it, smacking my face
on the shuffleboard court at the Sea Lion Motel
in Gloucester, MA. My parents out for the evening,

the neighbors' daughter stuck
a nubby motel washcloth full of ice
against my gums then rinsed my grated hands
and knees. In the morning
the tooth felt loose like my mother.

Shrine

Rosemary Zumpfe

My fingers read the braille
of blistered veneer.
Old mahogany headboard
rescued from the side of the road
now leaned against our garden fence,
peeling off in layers, needles of rain
slipped between, dissolving the glue.
How many stories are steeped
in its wood fibers, trim and curves,
dreams and deaths
tossed as lovers
in the wind of heated desire
burning the edges
to crow-black charcoal.

————

The surface is licked by flickers
of shade cast by the hackberry tree
half ripped away by a storm.
Yet it grows
in our backyard it grows
even as its rough branches
black as old umbilical chords
that sing and die away and fall
        and fall, and fall.
The wound in the trunk
aged to gray
weeps year after year.

In the cavity
I place the inherited
concrete elf with missing
toes and cracked arm
a fetish

summoning you
from your long distance
of doubtful sleep.

———•———

In ringings of crickets
I walk circles
around the white star magnolia
its roots twining around
the black the gold
cats wrapped in winding cloth
and buried inside of the rain
falling years ago.

The ash sky
flaps its wings
brushes my face
wind carries the distance
the train wailing
warnings
as it nears the crossing.

———•———

Do we betray our bodies ourselves
until our own betrayal seeps
like old oil
blood siphoned from the gash
cut into the flesh of earth.

———•———

Echoes from the park a block away
faint clang and toll
metal striking circling metal
retired men pitch
horseshoes
to rows of stakes
pounded into the ground.

The Untidy Season

My fingers read the braille
of each metal
rivet   plate   wire
each silver staple
that grips the edges
of morning and night
running across your skin
holding gristle and bone
a railroad
horseshoeing up your forehead
and curving down to your ear.

The afterward
of shining silver
scalpels slicing open
unearth the dark root and center
try to excise spidery legs
delicate tendrils
blossoming
under your skull.

Could my call, could any voice
have brought you back
from the maze of tunnels
burrowing deeper into
the dark
the cancer that darkened your face
that captured your mind

too deep for me
to reach inside
to heal you.

Nebraska Summer

Rosemary Zumpfe

I can't see the prairie from my fenced yard where I am pulling
weeds in summer heat, as if they are the ones who don't belong,
reclaiming this brick path between hosta and lily clumps.
Last night, lightning and rain stormed out electric lines,
shook us out of our beds and left our clocks missing four hours,

as if the immensity of sky that only Black Elk could
speak with was bellowing out our deepest secrets, and this
morning we are left without words big enough for land, for air,
for bird, for ant, for the small plot of ground where we might
touch what we could call the spirit that pulses under our feet,

that lives under the graves of concrete streets we spread
like an endless trail of blankets laid out for summer picnicing.
There is a pause that grows in the absence
of each golden bee or swish of swallowtail butterfly
that is beyond mourning. In the silence,

the mist rises, and the long breeze pulls its scarf
through the pine and linden and then dies, and I hold
my breath, listening for an answer, where to let go,
where to scatter the endless ashes. In each city garden,
we hoe and scrape, and in fields, farmers carve the earth

like sculptors shaping clay into sacred berths that can claim
this is mine, my way of living, while the wild prairie
grasses bob their heads in roadside gullies and stripes
of snakes and bellies of beetles slide over summer
dissolving it into dust bowls and winter awaiting their time

to blanket us over in gray or white. So worship
whatever you can, this pink morning, the branches torn
off maples, your hand that brushes a sea of black soil,
the scent of sage, the swollen river rising, flooding
the prairie, translucent cicadae shells clinging to twigs.

Wiping the Slate Clean

Rosemary Zumpfe

Rub the eraser large as a bar of soap
across each failed poem,
over drafts of letters
never sent, not honed
to perfection. Erase
the dried stalks of broken friendships
and old betrayals shriveled and cluttering
the sidewalks. Erase

every burnt dinner. Erase
each pan with blackened eggs
merged with metal. Erase
the weeds from the yard. Erase
the tears, erase the water
flooding up the Missouri.

Scrub the soft eraser's thinning
body on every seeping wound,
scab and ache. Let the rubbings
tumble around your feet like a mass
of narrow gray worms.

Gather the worms in your hands
like manna. Notice how, even now,
they hold the smell of corn silk,
the golden strands we strip off
and toss into the trash.

Contributors

Lucy Adkins grew up in rural Nebraska, attended country schools and the University of Nebraska, and received her degree from Auburn University in Alabama. Her poetry has been published in journals that include *Midwest Quarterly, Nebraska Territory, Northeast, South Dakota Review,* and *Concho River Review,* and the anthologies *Woven on the Wind, Times of Sorrow/Times of Grace, Crazy Woman Creek,* and *Poets Against the War.* Pudding House Press published her chapbook *One Life Shining: Addie Finch, Farmwife* in 2007. Her newest book, *Writing in Community: Say Goodbye to Writer's Block and Transform Your Life* (co-authored with Becky Breed), was released in April, 2013. She has led and worked with writing groups in the Lincoln area for many years.

Born in Denmark, **Margrethe Ahlschwede** lives in Lincoln, Nebraska. She graduated from Lincoln Northeast High School and earned college degrees from the University of Nebraska-Lincoln. She is professor emeritus of English, The University of Tennessee at Martin. Short stories and poems have been published in *CutBank, Prairie Schooner, Sou'wester,* and *Seattle Review.* She has been a quiltmaker for thirty years.

Susan Aizenberg has lived in Nebraska for over 25 years. She is the author of a full-length collection of poetry, *Muse* (Crab Orchard Poetry Series/SIUP Press), and a chapbook-length collection of poems, *Peru,* in Graywolf Press's *Take Three 2: AGNI New Poets Series.* She is co-editor, with Erin Belieu, of *The Extraordinary Tide: New Poetry by American Women* (Columbia UP), the first comprehensive, non-thematic anthology of poems by contemporary American women. Her poems and essays have appeared and are forthcoming in many journals, including *Spillway, Blackbird, burntdistrict, The Journal, Prairie Schooner, AGNI, The Laurel Review, Passages North, Third Coast, Chelsea, ONTHEBUS,* and *The Prague Revue.* She is Professor of Creative Writing and English at Creighton University in Omaha.

Sana Amoura-Patterson is the daughter of Palestinian immigrants but was born in Omaha, Nebraska. She graduated from the University of Nebraska Lincoln's Ph.D. English Program with an emphasis in creative writing and teaches full-time at Metropolitan Community College in Elkhorn, Nebraska, where she lives with her two children.

Mary Avidano of Elgin, Nebraska, is a former pastor and present poet originally from Mira Valley in central Nebraska. Her poems have appeared in *Nebraska Life* and elsewhere and now also on her website, maryavidano. com. Mary earned her degree in English at Loyola University of Chicago. Her chapbook of poems, *The Zebra's Friend & Other Poems*, was self-published in 2008. She is working on a second chapbook and recently completed *In the House of I Am*, a memoir of her early life—with, as she calls it, a seventy-five-year prologue. A United Church of Christ minister, Mary enjoys assisting her husband, Raymond, in his pastoral work and visiting their children and grandchildren.

Grace Bauer is the author of *Retreats & Recognitions, Beholding Eye*, and *The Women At The Well* as well as three chapbooks of poems and co-editor of the anthology *Umpteen Ways of Looking at a Possum: Critical & Creative Responses to Everette Maddox*. Her work has appeared in numerous anthologies and journals, including *Ploughshares, Poetry, Rattle, Natural Bridge, Blood Lotus, Midwest Quarterly*, and many others. She teaches in the Creative Writing program at the University of Nebraska-Lincoln.

Katie Berger was born and raised in Norfolk, Nebraska, and earned her BFA from the University of Nebraska at Omaha. Currently, she lives in Tuscaloosa, Alabama, where she works as a freelance writer and is a graduate teaching assistant in the University of Alabama's MFA in creative writing program. Her essays, stories, and poems have appeared in *ditch, Catch Up, otoliths, The Broken Plate, Plains Song Review*, and others. Her chapbook, *Time Travel: Theory and Practice*, is forthcoming from Dancing Girl Press.

Judy Brackett's stories and poems have appeared or are forthcoming in *The Long Story, Prairie Schooner, Other Voices, Squaw Valley Review, Alaska Quarterly Review, Sierra Journal, The Waterhouse Review, James Dickey Review, The Wisconsin Review, Sierra Songs & Descants* (Hip Pocket Press), and other publications. Her story "Mysteries" won a PEN Syndicated Fiction Prize and was broadcast on NPR's *The Sound of Writing*. Born in Fremont, Nebraska, she has lived in California's northern Sierra Nevada foothills for many years. She has taught creative writing and English literature and composition at Sierra College.

Debora Bray has worked for the State of Nebraska for the past twelve years. Prior to that, she worked in the broadcast industry. Debora says, "It seems I've always written poetry. The writing process often leads me to a broader understanding of a subject or occurrence. Most times, the thing I am thinking about when I begin to write does not end up being the subject of the resulting poem." Her poetry has previously appeared in *Illuminations, Fine Lines,* and *Tipton Poetry Journal.*

Becky Breed, a veteran educator, poet, and essayist, attributes the support of her writing community for inspiring her to craft the most honest and authentic writing of her life. She has an Ed.D. in Education, and in addition to helping develop a series of creativity workshops for women on the prairie, she has taught at the university level and served as principal at an alternative high school. Her book, *Writing in Community: Say Goodbye to Writer's Block and Transform Your Life,* co-authored with Lucy Adkins, was released in April, 2013.

Kate Brooke is a visual artist and poet. Her text-embedded images have been shown in more than twenty states, and she is the recipient of awards from venues including the Boston Printmakers and MONA. A resident of Lincoln since July of 1984, Kate grew up in Seattle and lived also in Arizona, Nigeria, Wisconsin, and Minnesota. She calls Nebraska her home.

Jill Burkey's work won the 2009 Denver Woman's Press Club Unknown Writers' Contest and received honorable mention in the 2009 Mark Fischer Poetry Contest. Her poems have appeared in *Pilgrimage Magazine, Soundings Review, Grand Valley Magazine, IMPROV Anthology of Colorado Poets, The Grand Junction Daily Sentinel,* in downtown Grand Junction's "Poetry in the Streets" project, and aired on KAFM 88.1 Community Radio. She is currently working on poetry for her chapbook, *Between Moons,* as well as a memoir about growing up on her family's four-generation cattle ranch in western Nebraska and her journey to find home since leaving the ranch. Jill earned a BA in English and business with endorsements in secondary education from Nebraska Wesleyan University. She currently lives with her husband and two children in Grand Junction, CO, where she works as a substitute teacher and Colorado Humanities Writers in the Schools resident.

Kathleen Cain is a Nebraskaradan with strong ties to her home town of Lincoln. Her poetry has appeared in many anthologies and journals, including most recently *Hospital Drive, Collecting Life: Poets on Objects Known and Imagined,* and *Feile-Festa.* Poetry is part of the liturgy of her religion, which is Wonder.

Nebraska-born, **Jill Carpenter** is a freelance writer who has published over 200 articles in the U.S. and Canada. She is a long-time member of the Lincoln Writers' WordShop. Writing, gardening, and grandchildren are her main addictions and distractions. She has lived and explored many states geographically and mentally but always returns to Nebraska. She has broken her own record by residing in Lincoln for the last 27 years. As an advocate for ADHD artists, she always has several projects going on at the same time. Currently she is finishing her first book of poetry, *From Pools of Sleep I Come*, and has been working on a series of rock 'n' roll suspense novels.

Shelly Clark Geiser is the author of *The Cockroach Monologues, Vol. 1* (Zero Street Books, 2011), a chapbook of insect persona poems. She is co-editor of an anthology of interviews and works by Nebraska writers, *Road Trip: Conversations With Writers*, (Backwaters Press, 2003), winner of two Nebraska Book Awards. Shelly's poetry has been anthologized in *Times of Sorrow, Times of Grace* and *Nebraska Presence: An Anthology of Poetry*. She has poems in *IMPACT: An Anthology of Short Memoirs* from Telling Our Stories Press and *Natural Bridge* (University of Missouri-St. Louis). Shelly received a BA from University of Nebraska, Kearney, and a Masters Degree at University of Nebraska, Lincoln. Shelly lives in Omaha, where she is currently at work on a YA novel, *The Room of Lost Dreams*.

Marilyn June Coffey is a national award-winning poet (Pushcart Prize) with more than 140 poetry publications in anthologies or serials, including journals such as *New American Review, Aphra, Sunbury*, and *Manhattan Poetry Review*. In 1991, Bandanna Books, Santa Barbara, California, published her book-length poem, *A Cretan Cycle: Fragments Unearthed from Knossos*. Charterhouse, New York, published her groundbreaking novel *Marcella* in 1973. Iowa State University Press published *Great Plains Patchwork: A Memoir* in 1989. Her prose has appeared in *The Atlantic Monthly, Natural History, American Heritage, Cosmopolitan*, been published by Associated Press, and been reprinted by Harper & Row, Macmillan, McGraw-Hill, and others. The University of Nebraska named Coffey a Master Alumnus for distinction in writing in 1977. Her papers are collected in the Marilyn Coffey Collection, Archives & Special Collections, University of Nebraska-Lincoln Libraries. Coffey is a retired English professor, having taught at Boston University, Pratt Institute, St. Mary's College in Lincoln, and Fort Hays State University in Hays, Kansas. Currently, she lives in Omaha.

Erin Croy's favorite poets are Anne Sexton and Jay-Z.

Cat Dixon teaches creative writing as an adjunct at the University of Nebraska, Omaha. She is the secretary of The Backwaters Press. Her work has appeared in *Sugar House Review, Midwest Quarterly Review, Coe Review, Eclectica*, and

Temenos, among others. Her poems were selected for a 2011 Lit Undressed event, part of the annual Downtown Omaha Lit Fest. Collaborating with military veterans and a Unitarian minister, Shawna Foster, she is putting together an anthology that will feature female veteran poetry and art.

Mary Marie Dixon, a visual artist and poet, is a graduate of the University of Notre Dame with an MA in theology and an MFA in English Creative Writing. She has published creative works in various periodicals and a collection of poetry, *Eucharist, Enter the Sacred Way*, Franciscan University Press, 2008. Her focus on women's spirituality and the mystics combined with the Great Plains and the spiritual power of nature makes for an eclectic mix. She has exhibited her visual work and accompanying poetry in galleries as she explores the visual and poetic intersection in her creative life.

A Nebraska native, **Eve Donlan** earned a BFA in poetry and MA in English from the University of Nebraska, Omaha. She and her husband are raising their four children in Omaha, where she teaches writing at UNO and Metropolitan Community College. Eve previously served on the board of the Nebraska Writing Center Consortium and on the Holy Cross School Board. She has participated in local poetry events such as Black and White and Read all Over: Ekaphrasis and Filling The Empty Room. Eve agrees with Isaac Bashevis Singer that "the wastepaper basket is the writer's best friend."

Marilyn Dorf grew up on the farm her great-grandparents homesteaded in Boone County, Nebraska, and cherished that "country upbringing." Her writing has appeared in various publications, including *Plainsongs, South Dakota Review, Willow Review, The Christian Science Monitor, Kansas Quarterly, Northeast, North Dakota Quarterly, Plains Song Review, Timber Creek Review, Nebraska Presence, Times of Sorrow/Times of Grace*, and *Crazy Woman Creek*. Her chapbook, *This Red Hill*, was published by Juniper Press in 2003.

Lorraine Duggin teaches English as a Second Language at Metropolitan Community College, where she also is a Consultant in the Writing Center. She is a Master Artist with the Nebraska Arts Council in Literature and in the Artists in Schools program for the Iowa Arts Council. She has published poetry, fiction, memoirs, and non-fiction in *Prairie Schooner, Nebraska Life, Nebraska Poets' Calendar, North American Review, North Atlantic Review, Short Story International*, among many other periodicals and anthologies, and her work has received several prizes, including an Individual Artist's Award in Poetry from the

Nebraska Arts Council, an Academy of American Poets' First Prize, a Mari Sandoz Prairie Schooner award for a short story, a Maude Hammond Fling Dissertation Fellowship from UN-L, and a nomination for a Pushcart Prize, among others.

Deirdre Evans was raised a Hoosier but moved to Omaha in 1978 to spin her adult life out in its Old Market and Midtown environs. She met husband Steven at the Nebraska Zen Center in 1997 and has lived happily ever after since then. She began poetry slamming with her husband at the OM Center in the Old Market in 2004 and became addicted to poetry slams, open mikes, chapbooks, and the company of poets. In 2009, she participated in the project Filling The Empty Room and is included in the book of poems of the same name.

Sarah Fairchild is the editor of Black Star Press, which publishes poetry books and the *Nebraska Poets Calendar*. She has taught English and writing at several Nebraska colleges and currently works as a mentor of highly gifted students for Lincoln Public Schools.

North Dakota native **Jackie Fox** has lived in Nebraska since 1980. When she moved here with her husband Bruce, a Lincoln native, she knew she was in the right place when she learned about Ted Kooser and Bill Kloefkorn. She was thrilled to interview both of them for *The Daily Nebraskan* and equally thrilled to take a UNL undergraduate poetry writing class with Hilda Raz. Fox holds a Bachelor's degree in journalism, and after a slight, two-decade delay, she has started work on her MFA. Her poetry has appeared in several now-defunct literary journals, including *Plainswoman* and *Whole Notes*, and *Rolling Stone* magazine. More recently, her poems have appeared in *Plainsongs, Conclave: A Journal of Character*, and *Touch: The Journal of Healing*. She is also a breast cancer survivor and author of *From Zero to Mastectomy: What I Learned and You Need to Know About Stage Zero Breast Cancer*, named a *Library Journal* Best Consumer Health Book in 2010.

Monica Fuglei jokes that she has had a twenty-four-year love affair with Nebraska. She received her BA and MA from the University of Nebraska at Omaha. Her first book, *Watching Her Poems Melting in the Rain*, was a collection of poetry written at age eighteen, and she has more recently been published in *Poetry Motel, The Rockford Review*, and *Red Ink*. Her most recent chapbook is *Gathering: 3 Works in Progress* (Morpo Press). Her zip code might be in Colorado, but her heart is still very much in Nebraska.

Kara Gall is a corn-fed, farm-bred Nebraska native who grew up in the Sausage Capital of Nebraska. An English instructor at Southeast Community College in Lincoln, her writing has appeared in the anthologies *Breeder: Stories from the New Generation of Mothers*, *Women Who Eat*, and *Why We Ride: Women Writers on the Horses in Their Lives*.

Megan Gannon's poems have appeared in *Ploughshares*, *Pleiades*, *Gulf Coast*, *Notre Dame Review*, and *Best American Poetry 2006* as well as on Verse Daily and Poetry Daily. Her chapbook, *The Witch's Index*, was published in 2012 by Sweet Publications. She has recently completed her second novel.

Gaynell Gavin is the author of *Attorney-at-Large* and *Intersections* (Main Street Rag Publishing). Her prose and poetry appear in many journals and anthologies, including *Bellevue Literary Review*, *Prairie Schooner*, and *Nebraska Presence* (Backwaters Press). She is a faculty member at Claflin University, where she teaches in the English and Politics and Justice Studies programs.

Karen Gettert Shoemaker is the author of *Night Sounds and Other Stories* (2002) and the novel *The Meaning of Names* (2014). Her work has been published in a variety of journals, including *Prairie Schooner*, *The London Independent*, and *The South Dakota Review*, and is anthologized in *A Different Plain*, *Times of Sorrow/Times of Grace*, and *Nebraska Presence*.

Crystal S. Gibbins holds a Ph.D. in English from the University of Nebraska-Lincoln. Her poetry has appeared in *Hayden's Ferry Review*, *Cincinnati Review*, and *H_NGM_N*, and her second chapbook, *SEA/WORDS*, is forthcoming from dancing girl press (2013). She is the founding editor of *Split Rock Review*.

Three sets of **Jane Goossen Wolfe**'s great-grandparents came to Nebraska and established farms in the 1880s. Her paternal great-grandparents were Mennonites from Prussia who came through Ellis Island and settled in southeast Nebraska. She graduated from Kearney State College with a degree in Special Education and taught at Lincoln Public for twenty-three years.

Teri Youmans Grimm is the author of *Dirt Eaters*, published by the University Press of Florida. Her writing has appeared in *Prairie Schooner*, *Indiana Review*, *Connecticut Review*, *South Dakota Review*, *Green Mountains Review*, *burntdistrict*, and *Homegrown in Florida: An Anthology of Florida Childhoods*, among other publications. She currently teaches in the low-residency MFA program at the University of Nebraska and lives in Florida where she hunts alligators and sings in a band.

Twyla Hansen's newest book of poetry (with Linda Hasselstrom) is *Dirt Songs: A Plains Duet*, winner of the 2012 Nebraska Book Award and finalist for the 2012 Willa Literary Award and High Plains Book Award. She is the author of five previous books of poetry, including *Potato Soup*, which won the 2004 Nebraska Book Award. Her BS (horticulture) and MAg (agroecology) are from the University of Nebraska-Lincoln. She is a creative writing presenter through the Nebraska Humanities Council and lives in Lincoln, where she maintains her wild, wooded acre as an urban wildlife habitat.

Allison Adelle Hedge Coke is a fellow of the Weymouth Center for the Arts & Humanities, Black Earth Institute (emeritus), and The Center for Great Plains Institute, with recent residencies at H. J. Andrews Experimental Forest (National Science Foundation), Hawthornden Castle and Lannan at Marfa, Hedge Coke has held two endowed chairs, is field faculty for the University of Nebraska MFA Program and Naropa University and serves as a Visiting Writer for the University of Central Oklahoma and the University of California, Riverside. Hedge Coke is a literary activist, works with disaster relief, incarcerated youth, elders, and in refugee and various other alternative populations in need, and founded and directs the annual Literary Sandhill Crane Retreat & Festival at the migration epicenter on the Platte River. She has authored seven books, including: *Dog Road Woman* (American Book Award for Poetry) and *Off-Season City Pipe* (Wordcraft Writer of the Year in Poetry), both from Coffee House Press; *Rock, Ghost, Willow, Deer* (AIROS Book of the Month, paperback 2014), memoir from the University of Nebraska Press; *Blood Run* (Wordcraft Writer of the Year for Poetry) from Earthworks of Salt Publishing; and *The Year of the Rat* (Grimes Press). *Burn* (MadHat) and *Streaming* (Coffee House Press) are 2014 releases in poetry and she is currently at work on *Red Dust*, a film documentary. Recently edited anthologies include, *Effigies* and *Sing: Poetry from the Indigenous Americas* (National Book Critics Circle Critical Mass Best of 2012, Wordcraft Circle Best Editing of 2012) and *Effigies II*, her ninth edited volume.

Carolyn Helmberger received her MFA in Creative Writing from the University of Nebraska in 2008. By day she works at the University of Nebraska Medical Center with the Endocrine fellows, by night she tries to collect her thoughts into poetry. She is an avid reader, a rabid Manchester United Football fan, and home to a small zoo of domestic pets. She has published in *The Chicago Quarterly Review*, *Controlled Burn*, and others.

Fran Higgins earned her BFA, a graduate certificate in Advanced Writing, and a Masters in English from the University of Nebraska at Omaha. Her work has appeared in *Plains Song Review, Celebrate, Slip Tongue, Les Femmes Folles: The Women 2011*, and *NEBRASKAland* magazine.

Samantha Hubbard grew up on a farm outside Huntley, Nebraska. Her favorite memories include riding her barrel horse, Sal, hauling irrigation pipe, and hearing the dinner bell ring. She now lives in Grand Island, Nebraska, with her husband, her children, and her cat. Her work has appeared in *Sierra Nevada College Review, Anode 2 Publishing*, and *The Plastic Tower*. In addition, her work appears in an anthology from New Wine Press called *Raw: A Poetic Journey*.

Joy Von Ill is earning her MFA in creative writing through Queens University in Charlotte, North Carolina. She lives in Omaha, Nebraska, with her cat, Virginia Wolfe. This is her first publication.

Natasha Kessler received her MFA from the University of Nebraska. She co-edits Strange Machine Poetry/Books and curates The Strange Machine Reading Series in Omaha. She is the author of the collaborative chapbook *SDVIG* (Alice Blue Books) with Joshua Ware. She has work featured in *SpringGun, inter|rupture, burntdistrict, iO Poetry, South Dakota Review*, and elsewhere. Her first full-length collection, *Dismantling the Rabbit Altar*, is forthcoming from Coconut Books (Spring 2014).

Maureen Kingston lives and works in eastern Nebraska. She is an assistant editor at *The Centrifugal Eye*. Her poems have appeared or are forthcoming in *Constellations, Emerge Literary Journal, Lily, The Meadowland Review, Psychic Meatloaf, Stone Highway Review*, and *Terrain.org*. For additional publishing history, see: http://mockingbird.creighton.edu/ncw/kingstonbib.htm.

Ruth Kohtz is a writer and performer from Lincoln, Nebraska. She earned a degree in Theatre Arts from Hamline University in St. Paul, Minnesota, and studied at the Jack Kerouac School of Disembodied Poetics in Boulder, Colorado. Before returning to Nebraska, Ruth regularly performed in the Riot Act Reading Series at the historic Turf Club in St. Paul and competed in the 2010 National Poetry Slam as a member of Punch Out Poetry. Her work has appeared in *The Midway Journal*, the *Hamline Fulcrum*, various chapbooks, and on the walls of bathrooms. She is currently a teaching artist with Nebraska Writer's Collective and Louder Than a Bomb youth poetry slam.

Karma Larsen didn't realize how much she loved Nebraska until she traveled to Europe and realized the pull this land had on her...how much she had come to love it and how much a part of her it had become. She says, "For the most part, the poems I write actually write themselves. It seems to me that poetry is, in some sense, what we do when words fail us...the everyday words of conversation, letters, prose. It's what comes out when we're witness to something far beyond us—beauty, sorrow, kindness—and all we can do is, as T.S. Eliot wrote, '...kneel/Where prayer has been valid.'"

Mary Logan spent many hours wandering around the country alone observing the landscape. She decided to go to college at age 39, majored in English and Medieval studies and won the Wood Memorial Prize for poetry while there. "I know that I can't separate writing from living, because it is how I try to make some meaning out of it all."

Judy Lorenzen grew up in Malcolm and Grand Island, Nebraska. She presently resides in Central City. She holds a BA, English; MSED, Community Counseling (LMHP); and MA, Creative Writing from the University of Nebraska-Kearney. She teaches high-school English, is a *Fine Lines* online editor, and was a past contributing writer for the *Heartland Gatekeeper* newspaper. Her work appears in *The Nebraska English Journal, Nebraska Poet's Calendar, Fine Lines, Times of Singing, Plains Song Review, Relief Literary Journal, The Platte Valley Review, Plainsong, Nebraska Life* magazine, and *Celebrate: A Collection of Writings by and About Women, Volume XVI*. She was the winner of the 2009 Nebraska Shakespeare Sonnet Contest.

Cathy Maasdam grew up in Cedar Bluffs, Nebraska. She is a life-long student and has earned Bachelor's degrees in education and music from the University of Nebraska-Lincoln. Maasdam is a musician, writer, and teacher whose poetry has appeared in *Fine Lines*. She currently lives in Lincoln, Nebraska, where she is employed by Lincoln Public Schools as a teacher for English Language Learners.

Kelly Madigan is the author of *Getting Sober: A Practical Guide to Making it Through the First 30 Days* (McGraw-Hill) and *The Edge of Known Things* (Stephen F. Austin State University Press). Her work has been published in *Prairie Schooner, Crazyhorse,* and *Terrain.org*. She is a recipient of a National Endowment for the Arts fellowship.

Ciara McCormack is a young dancer and poet with a BFA from Stephens College. She spent her first year out of school finding her feet in the prairie before moving on to bigger adventures in Seattle and abroad. She spends her time juggling numerous timecards, finding time for creative projects, and relaxing with her beloved. Ciara and her poetry strive to live in the expansiveness of miniscule movements and the humbling smallness of life under a big sky.

Sheryl McCurdy was born and lives in Cambridge, Nebraska. Trained as a nurse, she runs a busy coffee shop attached to her husband's pharmacy. They have three children.

Jean A. McDonough was born in Omaha, Nebraska, and now resides in upstate New York. She earned an MFA from Rainier Writers Workshop at Pacific Lutheran University, and she was the recipient of the 1995 Academy of American Poets Prize and a finalist for "Discovery"/*The Nation* and The Constance Saltonstall Foundation of the Arts Fellowship. Her work has appeared in *Dos Passos Review*, *Cold Mountain Review*, *The American Literary Review*, *Quarterly West*, *Tar River Poetry*, *Salamander*, *Bayou*, and *Poet Lore*, among others.

Deborah McGinn has her MA in English with a Creative Writing thesis and has been an IB 9 English teacher and Creative Writing teacher for Lincoln High going on 29 years. Most recently she organized the first Lincoln High student slam team, Louder Than a Bomb. The team placed third at the State Championship in Omaha. She is faculty advisor for the NCTE Superior Award-winning literary magazine at Lincoln High School, *Scribe*. Deborah published two chapbooks, *Self Unbound* and *To Go From Privacy*, and is working on a memoir about the quirky nature of dating. Deborah has been published in numerous magazines, including *English Journal*, *South Dakota Review*, *The Iowa Review*, *Ars Medica*, *Plainsong*, *Plains Song Review*, and *The Untidy Season*. She founded and hosts the Tuesdays with Writers series at the South Mill every first Tuesday of each month.

Cynthia McGowan is a writer, editor, and ESL teacher. Born and raised in Omaha, she studied English and linguistics at the University of Nebraska-Lincoln. Having spent the first 27 years of her life in Nebraska, she has since lived on the East Coast, in the Southwest, and amid the lush, dense foliage of Costa Rica. It was there that she wrote "Tarcoles River." Trading tornados for hurricanes, Cynthia lives in Tampa, Florida, with her partner of eighteen years and their three rescued dogs. She has a fictionalized memoir due out next year.

Jolene Moseman has taken creative writing classes at the University of Nebraska at Omaha and Metropolitan Community College. Her poetry has appeared in *Poetry Depth Quarterly, Plainsongs, The Metropolitan, Innisfree Magazine*, and other small presses.

Maria Mullinaux Cadwallader (formerly Lemon) moved from Florida to Lincoln, Nebraska, in 1968 and knew immediately that Nebraska was home. She worked as a social worker, attended graduate school, taught English at UNL, raised her children, and ran a small business. In 1998, she moved to a farm on a quiet road with little traffic, great neighbors, wildlife, gorgeous skies, frequent visits with family and friends, and the time and space to enjoy it all. She lives with her husband, Dean Cadwallader, and their dogs, cats, and horses and is the Valparaiso Public Library Director.

Nina Murray was born and raised in the western Ukrainian city of Lviv. She has been writing in English since 2003. Her poems and translations from the Ukrainian language have appeared in *Agni Online, Prairie Schooner, Midwest Poetry Review* and other publications. She is the translator, most recently, of Oksana Zabuzhko's novel *The Museum of Abandoned Secrets* (Amazon Crossing, 2012). After many years of living and working in Lincoln, Nebraska, she entered the US Foreign Service in 2011, and is currently serving as the Cultural Attache of the U.S. Embassy in Vilnius, Lithuania.

Charlene Neely's poetry has been published in *Plains Song Review; Songs For The Granddaughters; Dreams For Our Daughters; Times of Sorrow, Times of Grace; Nebraska Presence; Perceptions from Nowhere*; and others. She has done readings in coffee houses, nursing homes, and churches and visits various schools to teach poetry. She like to play with words like a three-year-old plays with blocks—shuffling them around, stacking up, knocking down and rearranging them until they suit her; she loves the sound, feel, and look of words. She is a member of Lincoln Chaparral Poets, Nebraska Chaparral Poets, Nebraska Writers Guild, and several other smaller and more informal writing groups, which all keep her muse on alert.

Molly O'Dell's second home is Nebraska, where the weather and people are real. She received her MFA from the University of Nebraska and her MD from Medical College of Virginia. She currently lives in southwest Virginia, where she works for the Virginia Department of Health as the Medical Director in the New River Valley. Some of her poems have appeared in *Plains Song Review*, *Platte Valley Review*, *JAMA*, and *Chest*.

Wendy Oleson is a Ph.D. candidate in creative writing at the University of Nebraska-Lincoln, where she serves as Senior Fiction Reader for *Prairie Schooner*. Her poems and stories have appeared most recently in *Rattle*, *The Baltimore Review*, *Copper Nickel*, and *Fifth Wednesday Journal*.

AJ Pearson-VanderBroek graduated from Peru State College in 2011 with a BS in language arts. Her work has been published in numerous online literary journals, including *Rose & Thorn*, *Breath and Shadow Magazine*, *The Legendary*, and *Short, Fast, and Deadly*. She writes horror and supernatural fiction under the pen name Matilda Loveshack. She lives in southeast Nebraska.

Amy Plettner lives fifteen miles from the city on a native 808-acre tallgrass prairie without a television or internet access, which gives her time to listen to the natural sounds around her: wind, birds, frogs, coyotes, crickets, and more wind. It's through this act of listening and solitude that she's inspired. Amy's poetry has been heard on NET Radio's *Poetry of the Plains*, with Bill Kloefkorn, and in numerous literary venues around Lincoln, Nebraska. She's a 2010 MFA graduate from the University of Nebraska low-residency writing program. Her first book of poetry, *Undoing Orion's Belt*, came out in 2011 from WSC Press. Writing has been an intimate part of her life for over twenty-five years.

Diane Raptosh has published three collections of poems, *Just West of Now* (Guernica Editions, 1992), *Labor Songs* (Guernica, 1999), and *Parents from a Different Alphabet* (Guernica, 2008). A professor of creative writing and literature at The College of Idaho and the recipient of three fellowships in literature from the Idaho Commission on the Arts, she has published widely in journals and anthologies in the U.S. and Canada. Her fourth collection of poetry, *American Amnesiac*, will be published by Etruscan Press in spring 2013. Diane Raptosh was born in Scottsbluff, Nebraska, and spent her earliest years there.

Caitlin Ray is currently a graduate student at the University of Nebraska at Omaha working towards her Master's degree in English. After living as an educator, actor, avid reader and not so secret writer in the Twin Cities, she is thrilled to be back in the Cornhusker state, where she grew up! Currently working as a teaching assistant at UNO, she also has a children's play, *Joey's Journey*, which was produced in libraries across southern Minnesota in April 2010.

Born in the Prairie State of Illinois, **Claudia Reinhardt** lived in Colorado, Boston, and Iowa before taking root in Nebraska. She holds degrees from Illinois Wesleyan University and Emerson College. Her work has appeared in various publications and anthologies, including *Contemporary Haibun Online*, *Fox Cry Review*, *Illuminations*, *Nebraska Life*, *Plains Song Review*, *The Wisconsin Review*, and *Writing in Community*. After a career in corporate communications, she now lives near a prairie and is a freelance writer, editor, and tutor.

Yelizaveta P. Renfro is the author of a collection of short stories, *A Catalogue of Everything in the World: Nebraska Stories*, winner of the St. Lawrence Book Award. Her work has appeared in *Glimmer Train Stories*, *North American Review*, *Colorado Review*, *Alaska Quarterly Review*, *South Dakota Review*, *Witness*, *Reader's Digest*, *Blue Mesa Review*, and elsewhere. She holds an MFA from George Mason University and a Ph.D. from the University of Nebraska-Lincoln.

Dee Ritter belongs to several writing groups. Her poetry has been published in *Avocet*, *Echoes*, *The Midwest Quarterly*, *Mid-America Poetry Review*, *Nebraska Poets Calendar*, *Nebraska Life*, *Plainsongs*, *Plains Song Review*, *Poppyseed Kolaché*, and other small journals. Her essays have appeared in *The Fence Post*, *Grit*, and *Rural Electric Nebraskan*, and her short story "The Summer of '45" appeared in the anthology *Friends, Stories of Friendship*.

Born in Michigan, **Lisa Roberts** studied English as an undergraduate at Princeton and did her English graduate work at The University of Virginia, with a focus on the Victorian poets, especially Gerard Manley Hopkins. She has taught literature and writing in Hong Kong, Charlottesville, Las Vegas, and, since 1993, in Lincoln, Nebraska, where she lives today and is writing poems again after a gap of many years. She says it was in Nebraska, at the age of 44, that she was reborn as a poet.

Marge Saiser's *Beside You at the Stoplight* (The Backwaters Press) won the Little Bluestem Award in 2010. In 2013, the University of New Mexico Press published her novel in poems, *Losing the Ring in the River*. Saiser's poems have appeared in *Chattahoochee Review*, *Cimarron Review*, *burntdistrict*, *Dos Passos Review*, *Rattle*, and *Prairie Schooner*. She has received several Nebraska Book Awards and a merit award from the Nebraska Arts Council. Her website is poetmarge.com.

Nancy Savery was raised on a farm near Dunbar in Otoe County, Nebraska, and has been a lifelong Nebraskan. She has been a member of Lincoln

Chaparral Poets and has won the Nebraska Mothers Poetry Contest on numerous occasions. She has been published in anthologies, *Nebraska Life*, chapbooks *Odyssey* and *Thoughts for All Seasons*, and her short stories have appeared in church publications. She is a member of Wachiska Audubon and serves as a docent and Board member at the Bess Streeter Aldrich Home in Elmwood. She has been a church choir member for 30 years and plays piano semi-professionally. She has 85 hours towards a UNL Bachelors in English.

Jeanne Schieffer works as the Corporate Communications and Public Relations Manager for the Nebraska Public Power District. She holds a Bachelor of Fine Arts from the University of South Dakota and a Master of Arts from the University of Nebraska–Kearney. Her poetry has been published in *The Carillon*, *The Reynolds Review*, and *Seasons to Come*. She has a 19-year portfolio of work published via utility business and trade magazines, newspapers, videos, and advertisements for radio and television. She is the author of the novel *Once You've Had It* and former publisher and editor of *Writing Works: A Quarterly Publication for Students and Teachers of Writing*. She is married, has two daughters, and lives in Columbus, Nebraska.

Barbara Schmitz's spiritual memoir, *The Path of Lightning: A Seeker's Jagged Journey*, was published from Pinyon Press in 2012. Earlier poetry collections include *What Bob Says* from Pudding House Press, *How Much Our Dancing Has Improved* (Backwaters), which won the 2005 Nebraska Center for the Book Award, and *How to Get Out of the Body* (Sandhills). She has been included in many Backwaters anthologies, including *The Nebraska Presence*, *Roadtrip*, and *Times of Sorrow, Times of Grace*. She's a Nebraska Arts Council winner and her poem "Uniforms" appeared in *South Dakota Review*, was chosen by Ted Kooser for his "American Life in Poetry" column, and was perfomed in the nude at the Omaha Lit. Festival (2011).

Morgan Songi grew up on a farm in western Nebraska. Her personal essays, short stories, and poetry have been published in literary journals in the U.S. and Canada. Her essay "Stormy Weather" was included in the anthology *Leaning Into the Wind: Women Write From the Heart of the West*. Experimental essays have been published in *Two Hawks Quarterly*, *Genre X*, and *Big Lucks*. She lives in Oregon and although she misses the drama of high plains storms, she appreciates not having to deal with sub-zero temperatures and whiteout blizzards. She's an enrolled member of the Red Cliff Band of Lake Superior Chippewas in northern Wisconsin.

Judith Sornberger has one book-length collection of poems (*Open Heart*, Calyx Books) and five chapbooks, including *Judith Beheading Holofernes* (Talent House Press), *Bifocals Barbie: A Midlife Pantheon* (Talent House Press), *Bones of Light* (Parallel Press), and *The Hard Grammar of Gratitude* (an interior chapbook published in *Poems & Plays*). Her most recent chapbook, *Wal-Mart Orchid*, was published in December 2012 and won the Helen Kay Prize from Evening Street Press. Sornberger is Professor of English at Mansfield University of Pennsylvania.

Sara Lihz Staroska is an English Instructor at Metropolitan Community College and a teaching artist through the Nebraska Arts Council. She is the author of six chapbooks, including *The Papier Mâché Repair Shop Opens for Business*.

Mary Stillwell is a native of Nebraska. She has studied writing in New York with William Packard, Erica Jong, and Marilyn Hacker. Stillwell has published widely in a number of poetry journals, including *New York Quarterly*, *The Paris Review*, *The Little Magazine*, *The Massachusetts Review*, *Confrontation*, and others, as well as in a variety of anthologies, including *Leaning into the Wind*, *The Decade Dance: A Celebration of Poems*, and *The Paris Review Anthology*. Her book of poems, *Moving to Malibu*, was published by Sandhills Press. Stillwell is coeditor of Nebraska Presence, an anthology of contemporary Nebraska writers published last year by Backwaters Press. Winner of a Merit Award from the Nebraska Arts Council (2006), she received her doctorate in Plains Literature from the University of Nebraska at Lincoln, where she is a lecturer. She and her husband, Frank Edler—who teaches philosophy at Metropolitan Community College—have two children: Wil and Anna.

Poet **Carla Stout** is the author of *Remote Fishing*. After forays in premedical studies and writing novels and short stories, Carla Stout came to poetry in the last decade. This time has been a furor of poetry for her. She has written poems on many subjects, including chapbooks and diverse projects. In addition to her writing, she is an award-winning gardener. She lives in Omaha.

Mary Strong Jackson lives in Santa Fe, New Mexico, where she continues her work as a poet and and freelance writer, and she is employed as a social worker in a psycho-social rehabilitation facility. Her work has appeared in various journals in the United States and England, and in the anthologies *At Our Core, Woman Writing about Power* (Papier-Mâché Press), *Times of Sorrow, Times of Grace* (Backwaters Press), and *In the Arms of Words* (Sherman Asher Publishing).

Tammy Trucks-Bordeaux is a mixed blood American Indian, English, and German poet who currently lives in Lincoln. Her poetry book, *Brought Back Safely*, was published in 2009 as part of the *Pudding House* chapbook series. She had also had poems published in literary journals such as *HazMat Review*, *Taproot Literary Review*, *The Haight Ashbury Literary Journal*, *South Dakota Review*, *The Rockford Review*, *Midwest Poetry Review*, and *Manna*. Three of her poems also appeared in *Times of Sorrow/Times of Grace: An Anthology of Nebraska Women Writers*. While attending the University of Nebraska-Lincoln, she won the Vreeland Award in Poetry and The Academy of American Poets Prize.

K. Denise Wally was born in Tulsa, Oklahoma. She has been writing poetry for 28 years. She also writes prose, mainly fantasy and science fiction. Other interests include gardening, biking, kayaking, travelling, music, astronomy, nature, art, and science. She has resided in Lincoln since 2001.

Susan Warren Utley lives and writes in the shadows of the Blue Ridge Mountains of Virginia. Memories of growing up in the Midwest provide much of the inspiration for her work. As her first stories and poems were written in her childhood home of North Bend, Nebraska, she is proud to have her first published works of fiction, and now poetry find homes with Nebraska-based publishers. In addition to writing, Susan is a co-founder and editor at Haunted Waters Press, home of the literary journal *From the Depths*.

Kathleene West is a retired professor from New Mexico State University, where she taught in the MFA Program and was Poetry Editor of *Puerto del Sol* for 15 years. She was a Fulbright Scholar in Iceland for two years. She has published ten books with Copper Canyon Press, Sandhills Press, and others, including a bilingual edition of her work, *Third World Romance/Romance Tercermundista* by Ediciones Catedral, Santiago de Cuba. Her latest book, *The Summer of the Sub-Comandante*, is available at amazon.com. A chapbook is forthcoming from Kattywompus Press. It is with deep sadness that the editors learned of the death of Kathleene West in July of 2013. She will be missed.

Born in Lincoln, **Rachel Naomi West** composed her first poem while on holiday in Bavaria at age four. Twenty-six years later, *The Untidy Season* is her first success in publication. She writes one or two short novels a year (plus innumerable poems) but is rarely able to discover their purpose. She doesn't really understand the term "literary fiction" and harbors a gentle animus towards NPR. She read too many misogynistic novels as a child and too little religious mysticism or history—a mistake she soon aims to correct.

She does not currently live with her beloved and supportive parents, Richard and Patricia. Her website (rachelwestbooks.com) offers a few poems and predictions.

Ruth Williams is a Ph.D. candidate in English Literature and Creative Writing at the University of Cincinnati. In addition to her chapbook, *Conveyance* (Dancing Girl Press, 2012), Ruth's poetry has appeared in *jubilat, no tell motel, H_ngm_n, alice blue, past simple, Bone Bouquet,* and *Bateau,* among others. Her critical work on feminism and women's literature has been published in *Michigan Feminist Studies* and *Tulsa Studies in Women's Literature* and is forthcoming from *The Journal of Popular Culture.* In 2011–2012, she was a Fulbright scholar in Seoul, South Korea.

Karen Wingett has lived in Nebraska for half her life. She grew up in South Dakota, taught English for many years, retired, and now travels the world with her husband. She has a BA in English from Yankton College and an MA in English from the University of South Dakota. Her poetry has been published in *The Mid-America Poetry Review, Nebraska Poets' Calendar, Nebraska Life Magazine, South Dakota Magazine,* and in the anthology *Times of Sorrow, Times of Grace.* She received a 2012 Independent Artist Fellowship in Literature from the Nebraska Arts Council.

Laura Madeline Wiseman has a doctorate from the University of Nebraska-Lincoln, where she teaches English. She is the author of several chapbooks, including *Branding Girls* (Finishing Line Press, 2011) and *She Who Loves Her Father* (Dancing Girl Press, 2012). Her poetry has appeared in *Margie, Feminist Studies, Poet Lore, Cream City Review,* and elsewhere. For more, www.laurama delinewiseman.com.

As a third-generation Nebraskan, **Julie Wrasse Van Winkle**'s ties are deeply rooted in Nebraska, as she was both born and raised in Lincoln, where she studied journalism and advertising at UNL. Julie is currently furthering her education in liberal arts at SCC, and she will be attending Doane College to complete her degree in Human Services. She has many creative passions, including poetry, drawing, painting, and jewelry design. Julie is employed at Kenexa, where she works in the logistics department. She is also a wife, proud mother of two amazing boys, Hunter and Evan, and owner of one silly Shih Tzu pup named Teddy.

Sandra Yannone received her Ph.D. in Creative Writing from the University of Nebraska-Lincoln, where she was an editorial assistant at *Prairie Schooner* during the editorship of Hilda Raz. Her poetry and book reviews have appeared in *Prairie Schooner, Ploughshares, Women's Review of Books, The Gay and Lesbian Review,* and *CALYX: A Journal,* among others. She currently directs the Writing Center at The Evergreen State College in Olympia, Washington.

Rosemary Zumpfe is a poet-artist teaching workshops in creative writing and intermedia arts in Lincoln, Nebraska. She has an MA in art from the University of Missouri-Columbia and a Ph.D. in English from the University of Nebraska. She expresses a feminist perspective through explorations of embodiment and the mythologies created in the written language of poetry and in the process of creating iconographical forms in visual art. Her poetic symbiotic approach challenges the separating of creativity into different disciplines, and her arts are an extension of the life cycle as a creative performance.

Editors

Heidi Hermanson has been published in *Midwest Quarterly*, *Hiram Poetry Review*, *PlainSpoke*, *Filling the Empty Room*, and elsewhere. She has been in many public art projects, such as "8 counts/24" (writers had 24 hours to write on a theme pulled randomly from a hat) and the benchmarks project, which featured brief inspirational quotes on bus benches throughout the city of Omaha. She organized the first Poets' Chautauqua at the State Fair and there released her first chapbook, *Midwest Hotel*. She has organized and directed four ekphrastic shows, which she describes as a marriage between visual art and poetry. In 2010 she won the Omaha Public Library's annual poetry contest and performed her winning work accompanied by Silver Roots, a New York-based violin and flute duo. She has read at the John H. Milton Conference in Vermillion, South Dakota, at the Bowery Poetry Club in New York City, at Tunes in the Town Square (which features poetry at the band's break) in Ralston, Nebraska, on the Kerry Pedestrian Bridge over the Missouri, and at the Roebuck Pub in England. In her spare time she hopes to open a library of maps to towns that do not exist and learn dialects of the seven-year cicada. In 2008 she received her MFA from the University of Nebraska at Omaha.

Liz Kay holds an MFA from the University of Nebraska, where she was the recipient of an Academy of American Poets' Prize and the Wendy Fort Foundation Prize. Her poems have appeared in such journals as *Beloit Poetry Journal*, *Nimrod*, *The New York Quarterly*, and *Sugar House Review*. Her chapbook, *Something to Help Me Sleep*, was published by dancing girl press in 2012. She lives and teaches in Omaha, where she is a founding editor of Spark Wheel Press and the journal *burntdistrict*.

Jen Lambert is a founding editor of *burntdistrict* and Spark Wheel Press. She holds an MFA in poetry from the University of Nebraska, and her work has appeared or is forthcoming in a variety of anthologies and journals, including most recently *The Los Angeles Review*, *The Raleigh Review*, and *Boxcar Poetry Review*.

Winner of the 2011 Nebraska Book Award for Poetry for her debut collection, *Cradling Monsoons*, **Sarah McKinstry-Brown** studied poetry at the University of New Mexico and the University of Sheffield, England. She's been published everywhere from West Virginia's standardized tests to literary journals such as *Chicago Quarterly Review*. Published in a number of poetry slam anthologies, her poems were featured alongside Poets Laureate Billy Collins and Ted Kooser in *The Spoken Word Revolution Redux*. McKinstry-Brown has taught performing and writing workshops in libraries, lockdown facilities, colleges, universities, and everywhere in-between. She currently teaches Creative Writing at the University of Nebraska at Omaha. When she's not reading or teaching, you can find Sarah in Omaha with her husband, the poet Matt Mason, and their two beautiful, feisty daughters. For more info, go to: sarah.midverse.com.

Lightning Source UK Ltd.
Milton Keynes UK
UKHW011239250221
379363UK00001B/91